D0191848

The Meaning of the Sacraments
By Monika Hellwig

Foreword by Rev. Robert W. Hovda

Pflaum/Standard
Cincinnati, Ohio 45231

Pflaum/Standard
Cincinnati, Ohio 45231
© 1972 by Monika Hellwig. All rights reserved
Library of Congress Catalog Number 78-178840
Printed in the United States of America
ISBN 0-8278-9056-7

In affectionate memory of
H. A. Reinhold

Foreword

The sacramental actions or realizations of the Church are in quite special need of "explanation" today for a number of reasons. One of the principal reasons for this strange need (to use words to explain that which communicates what cannot be expressed in words alone) is the historical fact that the sacraments have been overexplained in our comparatively recent Catholic tradition.

We who have built the automobile and the computer have found something wanting in the sacramental rites. Their world of poetry and symbol is a world of terror for the "let's call a spade a spade" girls and boys. We made of sacrament a mechanism that we could deal with—so we thought. We had it all explained, overexplained, in blueprints and production charts. You pulled the levers right and you hit the jackpot every time.

And then, suddenly, there was not enough left to satisfy the human heart's hunger for commitment, its thirst for spiritual meaning. The satisfactory trade relations we had established with the Almighty turned out—in the stress of living—to be something less than the stuff of commitment and of meaning. Now we need "explanations" of the sacraments to "de-explain," or, maybe, just to lead us from our neatly diagrammed and packaged world to the higher, clearer, more honest and encompassing world of mystery and grace.

The same cultural atmosphere that prompted us to shift our emphasis from the sacraments as signs to the sacraments as causes is an atmosphere unfriendly to contemplation. It is hard for most of us to look at and to see things. We don't have the time or the patience . . . or the interest. We see right away what things are *for,* what they can accomplish, how they can be *used.* And that's enough for us.

At least we thought so. Until the sacraments impinged upon our senses once again, in our language, and even sometimes with our ways. And we were all let down. Now we had to notice them, and to notice how little they really meant to us. Not only because an authentic "translation" of that sort involves more than words, but also because we find it hard to contemplate, to see things as they are and in themselves, to let ourselves relax in the world of poetry and symbol.

Theologian Monika Hellwig has written an illuminating and encouraging book about the sacraments of the Church. Illuminating—because she has a talent for sharing in lucid brevity her impressive biblical, historical, theological lore and insights. Encouraging —because she meets contemporary Catholics right where we are, with all of our baggage, and shows us how we are already on the way to a deeper, more authentic understanding of the sacred actions. This latter is perhaps an even greater talent, for it changes us, it moves us on, without berating us.

There is no implication here that most of what we have believed is a distortion, no attack to raise defences of self-preservation. Instead, there is appreciation of the gift of faith and of a fundamental vitality in the Christian affirmation which no crust of habit, no petrified formalism can completely suffocate or overcome. She works with what is there, in our piety and practice, and puts it in its best light—in context—as a part (distorted only if it is kept in rigid isolation) of the faith of the Church. So that, perhaps seeing something for the first time, we feel like saying, gladly, "I knew it all along!"

This is the way to teach. Dr. Hellwig addresses a sampling of real questions with respect to each of the sacraments. Her questions are real and her method is as instructive as her conclusions. I recommend it to fellow believers who desire a more satisfying experience in common prayer.

Robert W. Hovda

The Meaning of the Sacraments

Introduction

This book has grown out of lectures, workshops and discussions with diocesan, parish and parents' groups. Experience has shown that the questions many Catholic adults entertain about the meaning of the sacraments today are not questions that were answered by the catechism they learned as children. They are not, moreover, the questions theologians usually argue about today. They are "gut-level" questions about personal experience and personal responsibility and the personal effort to make sense of life.

The questions people are asking are mostly the type of questions they must themselves answer by the way they live their faith commitment. These are not questions that lend themselves readily to a textbook answer. Yet many people have complained that they do not have a sufficient basis for understanding how to discover and create answers for themselves. It seems that this is largely because we have in the sacraments a whole language of gestures, signs, symbols, stories, allusions, and we have long ago forgotten the vocabulary and grammar of the language. To understand what is being expressed, we have to try to remember the language.

The original language of the sacraments grew out of life experience and its repercussion on ordinary flesh and blood people, just as any language grows. This book attempts to lead the reader back to the experiences, to relive them in imagination and make them his own. The book, therefore, picks up the biblical themes and indicates briefly what Christian experience has made of these biblical themes. From that point each chapter considers the implications of some common and urgent questions that Catholics encounter today about sacramental practice, in the light of the traditional devotion and of theological reflection.

It may be well to make it clear at the outset that this book does not attempt a theology of sacraments in any systematic or conventional sense. It omits many questions that theologians consider important because they are questions that do not seem to be troubling committed Christians who are not theologians. For those who want to pursue their study into sacramental theology in the strict sense, some suggestions for reading are made at the conclusion.

In order that the chapters may read easily and smoothly, acknowledgment of sources and reference to authors and books that may be of help, are made not in the text but in notes after each chapter. What cannot be acknowledged in the notes is the author's extensive indebtedness to inspirational Christian teachers and friends who have shared their insights and living commitment as Christians, to the participants in many adult programs who persevered in asking searching questions that were difficult because they were so simple, and to the exceptional kindness of Jewish friends who have opened up vistas of meaning in the biblical symbols by their warm manifestation of the community way of life that is Israel.

Baptism and the community commitment 1

Very many Catholic Christians have problems about baptism today. Most of these revolve around the baptizing of infants. People want to know what difference it really makes whether a child has been baptized, and whether he ought not to have the opportunity to grow up and find out what religion is all about before getting himself involved in any church obligations. Young people frequently want to know by what right others have made a commitment on their behalf about which they were never consulted. Parents sometimes want to know whether it is important to have children baptized as quickly as possible, since infant mortality, though rapidly declining, is still a reality among us.

When people ask these questions, they often want the answer much more briefly and dogmatically than it can be given. The purpose of a book such as this is not to give easy answers but to sketch in the background by which a person can formulate the questions in such a way that he can answer them himself.

As far as baptism is concerned, the most important part of that background by far is the biblical theme of water and new birth out of which the community action of baptism has grown. Another significant part of the background is the history of the Christian custom of baptizing and the Christian explanations of the action. A third necessary element of the background is the development of the Christian understanding of sin and redemption and of the Church as the way of redemption.

The biblical theme of water has a long perspective. In Genesis God creates not out of nothing but out of chaos, and chaos is represented by waters and darkness. One has the impression of a dark turbulent ocean in a storm, completely beyond control, inspiring terror and despair, with powerful forces of destruction sucking down and crushing all possibilities of life and order and meaning. We are told that God masters or subdues the waters of chaos, separates earth and sky, draws out some dry land where things can grow, and assigns the waters their boundaries. It is rather difficult to feel the full emotional impact of the poetic image of the waters of chaos, unless you have at some time been close to drowning, or had to watch someone drown, or been in real danger in a boat at sea. Suddenly the whole of your world, the whole of reality is overwhelmed with chaos and you are quite powerless no matter how intelligent, well educated, rich or famous or well-connected you might be. The ocean respects none of these claims to special consideration. It simply wipes out everything that culture and effort have built.

There are, of course, other ways in which the fruits of men's labors can be destroyed utterly. After the creation story, in which the world is born out of the waters of chaos in a kind of fresh innocence, Genesis gives a story of everything being inundated again because of the overwhelming wickedness of men. Genesis does not say that men are heading toward a holocaust of nuclear destruction because of greed and lust for power and mutual mistrust. Neither does it say that there is an ecological danger that men will exterminate themselves through sheer selfishness. Genesis says that things can get so bad (and indeed have done so) that not even God himself, who first brought the world out of chaos, will any longer hold back the waters of chaos that once again overwhelm all the efforts of men. But God gathers a representative few and invites them into an ark, a specially-made ship, that is able to ride the waves of chaos. Entering the ark is a commitment to a special relationship to God. Those who do so are, so to speak, reborn out of the waters of chaos into a new world and a fresh beginning. That is why immediately upon their exit from the ark, God spells out for them the terms on which that fresh beginning is possible, namely, a deep and universal respect for life.

In the history of Israel there is another great passing through the waters of chaos and into new life. From the horror and helplessness and despair of the sojourn in Egypt, the book of Exodus tells us, Israel passed through the Red Sea at the invitation of God and came out on the other side a new nation, while the Egyptian oppressors perished in the waters of chaos. Every situation of helplessness, engendering a slave mentality in the oppressed, is indeed the return of the waters of chaos. But out of that chaos God calls men to a new beginning as His people, the community built from the response to His call. In the thinking of Israel and in the stories of the Pentateuch, the great passing through the waters is not completed after the emergence from the Red Sea. There is still the crossing of the Jordan, another passing out of a relative state of chaos into the Land of the Promise. In a sense, the Jordan crossing is one that is forever in the future. There is always another crossing before the Promise of God for the new creation, the fresh and sinless start, is fulfilled. But meanwhile, each crossing commits each person to membership in the people of God, which is a people committed to that new beginning in response to God's call.

Israel has, through the ages, baptized converts who have come from among the nations seeking membership in Israel as the People of God. In such a baptism the newcomer recapitulates in his person, in a dramatic reenactment, the sacred history of Israel. He is immersed bodily in waters symbolizing the primeval chaos, the flood-time wickedness of men, the bondage of Egypt, and the river Jordan that bars the way to the Promised Land. Symbolically, he goes through the passage from death to life which the people have made so many times. He goes through the drama of "catching up" with them. The emergence from the waters initiates him into the people, and into their way of life and their commitment in response to the call of God to a fresh start. By passing through the waters in the ceremony he also accepts the conditions of the Sinai Covenant in addition to those of the covenant God made with Noah.

John the Baptist, the Gospels relate, appeared as a prophetic figure on the banks of the river Jordan, proclaiming, "Reform your lives! The reign of God is at hand" (Mt. 3, 2.) When he is asked what the conditions are this time for the new rebirth of the people of God out of the prevailing chaos, for the imminent entry into the Promise of God, his answers are terse, simple, obvious and concrete (Lk. 3,10-18). But John himself is bewildered when his cousin Jesus presents himself as a candidate for this baptism. The explanation given is that Jesus will "fulfill all of God's demands" (Mt. 3,15). We are being told that Jesus is to lead a new passage out of the waters of chaos by going all the way down into them himself. By John's baptism he looks back over the history of his people, dramatically making it his own, and looks forward to the final crossing of Jordan into the Promise of God which he himself is to lead.

The evangelists refer to the theme of the waters of chaos several times. They speak of having seen Jesus walking on the threatening and stormy waters of the lake, which calmed down as soon as he got into their boat with them (Mk. 6,48-51). They recall his saying with reference to his forthcoming death that he yet has a baptism to undergo and is in suspense until it is over (Lk. 12,50). The appendix to John's Gospel puts the disciples in a boat out on the lake, making for the shore, but the Risen Christ is already on the dry land, waiting to welcome them with a meal that he has prepared (Jn. 21,1-14).

This brings us to the second part of the background to the contemporary understanding of baptism: the history of the Christian custom of baptizing and the Christian explanations of the action. In the New Testament the apostolic community makes it quite clear that entrance to the community is by baptism into the death and resurrection of Jesus. Those who did not live through these events as they happened in history are to "recapitulate" in a dramatic celebration of the community the experience of rebirth from despair to hope, from crushing defeat and failure to the explosion of undreamed-of new possibilities in life.

The First Letter of Peter speaks of a new birth to

hope which is based on the resurrection of Jesus Christ from the dead, a birth to an imperishable inheritance and a salvation which is yet in store for the Christians (I Pet. 1,3-5). It is not yet fully revealed because they are still in the era of struggle, in the moment of the crossing from death to life (I Pet. 1,6-21). But they should have hope and the courage to live radically different lives, staking everything on the promise of the resurrection, because they are already reborn from indestructible seed, the risen Jesus, who, for their rebirth, brings them together as a people, God's people (I Pet. 1,22—2,10).

Paul's writings underscore and develop these themes. Baptism means being plunged into the experience of the death of Jesus, so as to be raised by the Father to a new life, a radically new life in which all kinds of slavery and confusion and despair are left behind (Rom. 6,1-14). An important aspect of that radical newness is that all who are baptized into Christ are heirs in him of the common destiny of God's promise, so that there can be no more discrimination between races, sexes or classes of people (Gal. 3,26-29). That is what baptism means to Paul, and that is probably why he is convinced that baptism is simply the entrance into a community task that will be a lifetime struggle (Col. 2,9—4,6.).

We know from the endings we now have to Matthew's and Mark's gospels that the apostolic community was convinced that the risen Jesus expected them to go out and draw men and women of all nations into the new community, living a radically new kind of life in the world (Mt. 28,19-20. Mk. 16,15-16.).

In the early centuries of the church the community grew in numbers because adult persons, sometimes whole families, saw the miracle of the new life and the ecstatic new hope, and they believed in the saving power of the death and resurrection of Jesus, and were baptized. Their children might be baptized along with them but the ceremony of baptism was set up for adult converts. It supplied a vivid outward sign of their conversion, their entrance into the community and the community's acceptance of them in the common life and destiny and endeavor.

We know that the ritual of baptism came to be spread out over a time of initiation known as catechumenate, lasting perhaps months, perhaps years, as has also been the case in modern times in missionary situations. It was not always and everywhere the same, but it did always involve a preliminary explanation of what was required of one who entered the Christian community: extensive instruction in scripture, expositions of the creed and the Lord's Prayer, some sort of assessment of the sincerity of the catechumen's conversion, and a time of intensive common prayer. While adult baptisms were the norm, it was common practice to celebrate them at the Easter Vigil.

For some centuries, even those who had been born into Christian families and raised as Christians had a clear appreciation of the newness of the Christian way of life and the radical nature of the conversion celebrated by a baptism, because they witnessed each year the final stages of preparation and the actual baptism of adult converts. With the eventual numerical success of the Church, this was no longer true. For very many centuries in the West, most of us have not been aware of Christian life as being special or different or new We have not thought of the Christian commitment as something very radical, calling for an act of most extraordinary human freedom. As a matter of fact, we have thought of it as the ordinary pattern of life into which people are drawn without much choice or reflection.

The liturgy of the Catholic Church has tried to offer an opportunity for this realization to break in on individual Christians who were open to it, in the Lenten readings and observance and in the Easter liturgy, especially in its restored form. The Lenten and paschal seasons have maintained the catechumenate themes of enlightenment, conversion, scrutiny and public commitment. They have offered Christians, and do so today, a new crossing of the Jordan, a new plunging into the mystery of the death and resurrection of Jesus for a rebirth to new life, new hope, new community, new authenticity. They offer the Church community as a whole a dramatic liturgical reliving of its foundation experience and an opportunity for a rebirth to be the kind of community that strives to realize the vision of Jesus.

Those of us who were baptized in infancy can pick up the catechumenate experience later by progressive realization of and entrance into the death and resurrection of Jesus, and a progressive realization of how extraordinary a truly Christian life is. But here there is a very genuine dilemma. Although it is possible for us to achieve this realization, it is a constant exercise of a very radical human freedom. It can by no means be forced or required of anyone, for that is the opposite of freedom. One cannot force another to make a free choice or to undertake a free commitment. Therefore, there is no way of guaranteeing that all those baptized in infancy will undergo a Christian conversion and personally enter into the death and resurrection of Jesus. Not even the best Christian family in the world can guarantee this, nor the most actively involved parish, nor the most devoted pastors, nor the most lively and

chapter one

relevant liturgy, nor the best-staffed Catholic schools. As we are beginning, once again, to realize this, many Catholic parents, teachers and catechists are asking themselves why we baptize in infancy at all, and what their responsibilities are to the children and young people who have been baptized. The question goes back to the origins. People started baptizing their babies from an intuitive sense that it was good and sensible to bring them into the community of Christians as soon as they were born and to offer them a hearty welcome there. Not only among Christians but among all peoples of the world it has been customary to want to celebrate a birth with a religious ceremony, and usually this is a ceremony of welcome into the community. Christians, like other people, made a habit of doing this first and reflected on the theological explanations much later.

This brings us to the third aspect of necessary background in solving contemporary questions about baptism: the Christian understanding of sin and redemption and Church. In earlier centuries of the Church's history, people were not much inclined to ask what they were being redeemed from, because that seemed so obvious. Sin to them was not an abstraction. Oppression of the poor, hatred, rivalries, wars, greed, suspicion, frustration and fear made the experience of unfreedom or alienation very evident in people's lives. Redemption, which means liberation, was something they had experienced very immediately and concretely through their contact with the community of the followers of Jesus. These people lived differently and gave one another so much support in doing so that even in circumstances of bitter persecution by outsiders or in times of personal failure, bereavement or distress, the joy of the resurrection was evident among them. They always had the forward thrust of a great and confident hope in the future total fulfillment of the promise of the resurrection. The way that redemption was made presently available and evident was through and in the community of the followers of Jesus who lived that way.

This, of course, is why the Church grew to such vast numbers so fast. People really saw salvation and wanted it. As long as the contrast between the distress and frustration of the world and the presence of redemption in the community of believers was evident, baptizing infants was also self-explanatory. It was desirable to draw them into the community of redemption even before they themselves were aware of the state of unredemption into which they were born.

At times, however, when people have been less aware of sinfulness and the need of redemption, the baptism of infants has not been so obvious. At such times people have asked the wrong questions. They have asked how an innocent infant can be guilty of other people's sin and can need forgiveness for it. It is not a question of guilt in the sense of blameworthiness but of responsibility in the sense of having to answer with a solution to the existing problem. What Christian baptism asserts is that no one can really offer a solution and live sinlessly in the world alone, but that through the death and resurrection of Jesus it has become possible and not futile for the community to strive together to do this. In the baptism of an infant the community of believers pledges itself to welcome him into that common effort and not leave him to struggle against unredemption alone. The faith of the community reaches out to him, although he does not understand what it is all about.

Most young people in Christian communities accept

this welcome as an invitation which they do not question too much. They learn a more or less Christian way of life rather unthinkingly, because it does not occur to them to do anything else. They may or may not penetrate deeply much later into the implications of the death and resurrection of Jesus. If they live their whole lives as "fellow travellers," leaning on the support of others for some consolation and meaning in life, and using their religion as a guide to a more or less moral life, there is, of course, nothing lost. If they glimpse in one dimension or another what the redemption is about and live this one aspect—whether in the reconciliation of races and classes, or in grasping the redemptive nature of suffering in their own lives, or in compassion for the poor and deprived, or in passionate commitment to social justice by changing the structures of society, or by a detachment that puts people above things and happiness above status, or in whatever way—much has been gained, even if these young people do not turn into churchgoers.

In societies as diverse as ours and times as rapidly changing as ours, however, there are some young people who do not take their being Christians for granted and do not discover joyfully what Christianity is about. Instead of seeing baptism as the gateway to salvation and great personal freedom, they see it as doom and captivity. This could be due to over-anxious, over-conscientious efforts by adults at Christian education. In childhood, a person should be allowed to take many things for granted, to be more a receiver than a giver, and to be free from adult responsibilities and burdens. At adolescence, the young person may be invited to the world of adult responsibilities and commitments, but he cannot become an adult unless he is left free to make his own commitments. That means he must be left free to remain uncommitted for a while. It also means he must be left free to make commitments which may be different from those his parents and teachers envisage for him. It means we should expect that some young people raised in Christian families will not choose to make a personal Christian commitment. At a given time in history these may be few or many. To attempt to coerce them by fear does not make the Christian community stronger but much weaker.

It will be easier for all of us to penetrate further into the death and resurrection of Jesus and its many far-reaching implications in our secular lives, if we consistently understand the baptism of infants as an invitation in which the community accepts an obligation towards those baptized but cannot impose any obligations on them without their subsequent free and adult commitment of themselves to the common task of redemption. This is very difficult for most of us to do in practice because we ourselves are not wholly redeemed but on the way to redemption, and therefore we seldom respect the freedom of another person as Jesus and the Father do. It has to be our constant endeavor to learn that respect.

Notes

The questions concerning the traditional concepts of original sin are not discussed in this chapter because they are covered in Chapter VII of the author's earlier book, *What Are the Theologians Saying?* (Pflaum Standard, 1970)

The rite itself is not discussed here because the new text with brief explanations is easily available from the Liturgical Press, Collegeville, Minnesota, in a pamphlet entitled *The Rite of Baptism.*

The biblical themes taken up in this chapter are very fully described in the first six chapters of Jean Danielou, *The Bible and the Liturgy*, from the University of Notre Dame Press. A brief account of the more important historical facts and their theological implications is available in Charles Davis, *Sacraments of Initiation*, published by Sheed & Ward, 1964.

Confirmation and the personal dimension 2

Concerning confirmation, most reflecting adult Catholics today seem to have two questions: what specific difference does this sacrament really make and at what age ought it to be received? Again, it will be well not to attempt any immediate answer to these practical questions, but to sketch in the underlying biblical theme of Spirit, the Christian history of confirmation, and the connection with the doctrine of grace and the salvation of the individual.

The theme of Spirit appears at the very beginning of the Bible. In the Genesis account of creation, the breath of God hovers over the waters of chaos. The Hebrew word we translate as spirit has a rich range of meaning: breath, wind, sign of life, communication of life. In the second creation story (Genesis 2), the narrator makes a special point concerning the creation of man: God breathes his own breath into man, and that is how man becomes a living being. In the story of Noah and the flood, God sends a wind across the earth and the chaotic waters subside so that the world is reborn (Genesis 8). Again in Israel's crossing of the sea of reeds into freedom, the narrator of Exodus tells us that the Lord swept the sea with a strong east wind all night and turned it into dry land (Exodus 14,21). The Hebrew scriptures also give us some powerful stories of the wind or breath of God in relation to individuals. Moses meets God at the top of the mountain in the midst of a storm (Exodus 19,18). Elijah, on the other hand, goes to the top of the mountain to find that God is not in the strong and blustering wind nor in the earthquake nor the fire, but in a tiny whispering sound (I Kings 19,9-13). Both Moses and Elijah were called to special and difficult missions in these incidents. The vision in which Ezekiel was called to a prophetic role was also heralded by stormy winds (Ezekiel 1,4).

When Ezekiel and others write of being possessed by the spirit of the Lord, or led by the spirit, they most often seem to refer to the spirit of prophecy, that is, the power and courage and clarity of vision to speak the truth of God into the confusion and deception of some evil situation among men. The stories of the great prophets make it very clear what a hazardous and demanding vocation this is. Prophets are often rejected and not infrequently killed as public malefactors. It is clear in the scriptures that the extraordinary personal freedom that makes it possible for the prophets to give this kind of witness is due not to some special personal talent or virtue in them, but to God's gift of his own utterly free spirit which He has breathed into or communicated to them.

When we read of the spirit breathing or the wind blowing in an event relating to the whole people, it seems always to be connected with a moment of rebirth, of new life, of passing through some dark death to greater life. The most striking symbolic presentation of this is Ezekiel's vision of the great plain covered with dead bones (Ezekiel 37). The Lord gives Ezekiel the explanation of the vision: His people have lost hope and are as good as dead but He will once again put His own spirit into them and they shall live.

The New Testament takes up this theme, first in relation to Jesus himself, and after his death and resurrection in relation to his followers. Luke tells us that Jesus was conceived by the power of the spirit or life-giving breath of God (Luke 1,35). He also tells us of several representative figures who were possessed by the spirit of God and enjoyed the prophetic freedom and clarity of vision to recognize the divine breath in Jesus: John and Elizabeth (Luke 1,41-43), Simeon (Luke 2,25-32), and Anna (Luke 2,36-38).

Luke's recital continues with the observation that, at the baptism by John, the spirit of God descended on Jesus visibly (Luke 3,21-22) and then led him into the desert to the solitary confrontation with the ancient tempter over the nature of his mission (Luke 4,1-13). In the power of the spirit or breath of God Himself, Jesus returned to Galilee and began his preaching (Luke 4,14), identifying himself with a quotation from Isaiah, "The spirit of the Lord is upon me . . . to bring good news to the poor, to proclaim freedom to the unfree, new vision to those who cannot see, liberation to those who are imprisoned . . ." (Luke 4,18-19).

When Luke tells us of the successful first mission of the seventy-two disciples, he adds that Jesus rejoiced that they had really received the life-giving breath of the freedom of God that he had communicated to them (Luke 10,21).

John's gospel provides further reflections on the freedom of the spirit of God. To receive the spirit is to be born to new life, for spirit begets spirit and those who are born of the spirit have the freedom of the wind (John 3,5-8). Jesus claims to usher in a time when people will be able to worship the Father not slavishly with rules and rituals that they do not understand but in spirit and truth (John 4,23-24).

When it has become clear that the mission of Jesus will end as prophetic missions have usually done, John gives us the spirit or breath-of-God theme again. Jesus explains to his followers that it is necessary for him to go into this death, but through it the Father will give them his own breath of truth and life and freedom (John 14,16), and in that spirit they will gradually understand what he has done and said and suffered (John 14,26). The breath of God in them by which they will live will give witness to Jesus, so that they will understand and will become witnesses to others (John 15,26-27). If Jesus does not die this death, the life-giving breath of God, the spirit of prophecy, will not take possession of his followers, for it is by his death that he breathes the life of the Father into them (John 16,7). It is his death that is the definitive confrontation of God's merciful and saving truth with men's defensive, threatened sinfulness; that death will shatter their vision but quietly the spirit which he communicates to them will bring them to understanding and they will see him again (John 16,8-28). In reporting the appearance of the risen Jesus to the assembled gathering of his disciples, John tells us he commissioned them to be his witnesses and breathed on them, communicating to them the spirit (John 20,21-22).

In the Acts of the Apostles it is clear that the gift of the spirit of Jesus, the life-giving breath of the Father, is made by Jesus to the community of his followers, the assembly or church, and that it is through the community that the gift of the spirit is subsequently communicated to new believers. The classic story is that of Pentecost with the strong rushing wind that took possession of the members of the community with tongues of fire (Acts 2,1-4). The response of these disciples in giving witness was so startling that Peter's sermon could claim the fulfillment of what had been promised in the Hebrew scriptures by Joel, that the spirit of God would be poured out on all mankind so that prophecy would become a very common phenomenon (Acts 2, 14-21).

It is in the continuing narrative of the Acts of the Apostles that the Christian history of confirmaticn begins. As the community of believers takes shape after Pentecost, definite patterns develop for the reception of newcomers into the community. The ceremony of baptizing them "into the death and resurrection of Jesus Christ" is accepted as a necessary step. However, there are several references in the Acts of the Apostles to the laying on of hands. For instance, after the conversion of many people in Samaria, Peter and John went there and laid hands on those who had been "baptized in the name of the Lord Jesus because the Spirit had not yet come upon any of them." When the two Apostles laid hands on them, the coming of the Spirit upon them was so clearly evident that an unbeliever named Simon offered the Apostles money if only they would give him the power to bring the Spirit upon people by laying on of hands (Acts 8,14-19).

A little later in the Acts of the Apostles we are told that Paul laid hands on the first believers in Ephesus and they spoke in tongues and prophesied, so that everyone could see quite clearly that they had received the gift of the Spirit.

The early Christian community seems to have been

Confirmation and the personal dimension   23

well aware that the Spirit was given to the Church community not that the Church might control the Spirit but that the Spirit which breathes where it will might direct the Church. We are told that Peter was called once from Joppa to Caesarea. A centurion named Cornelius and his whole household wanted to hear the gospel of Jesus from him. They were, of course, gentiles, and at that time the only followers of Jesus were still all Jews. No sooner had Peter given his account of the good news than the Spirit was poured out on them and they were speaking in tongues and glorifying God. It was at this point that the Jewish believers realized they could not withhold baptism from the gentiles since God himself had poured out His Spirit upon them (Acts 10). When Peter has to explain this to the community at Jerusalem, he recalls that Jesus himself once said, "John baptized with water, but you will be baptized with the Holy Spirit" (Acts 11,16).

After these introductory accounts of laying on of hands to obtain the gift of the Spirit, and of spontaneous baptism of the Spirit, the Acts of the Apostles and the letters of the New Testament very frequently explain some particularly courageous action, some extraordinary apostolic success, some sermon that moved many listeners to believe in Jesus Christ, by saying that those who did these things acted in the Holy Spirit or were sent by the Holy Spirit. It would seem that they saw the Holy Spirit in people whenever there was evidence of courage, insight, power or joy that exceeded what was humanly possible.

In our own day many Catholics have questions about the Pentecostal movement. At its best it is a repetition of this experience of the early Church, where a community of believers prays and lives with such sincerity that, again and again, individuals are seized by the

Spirit of God, the breath of Jesus, and it is evident how much they are living by the guidance of the Spirit because of extraordinary manifestations of courage, insight, power and joy. Pentecostal groups describe the experience with the expression that Peter said he remembered Jesus as using, "baptized with the Holy Spirit."

Of course, the apostolic community was well aware that excitable and hysterical people may also delude themselves that they are possessed by the Spirit of God when they are merely "high" on the stimulus of some kind of mass hypnotism. Today, as in the early days, there has to be some shrewd, common-sense assessment as to what spirit it is that guides people's lives and actions. Today, as in the early days, there is really only one basic criterion: "You can tell a tree by its fruit" (Mt. 12,33). The letters of the New Testament are full of advice as to how one should judge the spirit by the actions that flow from it. Probably the briefest and most helpful passage is one in Paul: "The fruit of the spirit is love, joy, peace, patient endurance, kindness, generosity, faith, mildness and chastity" (Gal. 5,22). A longer and very searching discussion is offered in I Corinthians, Chapters 12-14.

After the testimony of the New Testament we seem to lose sight of the history of this laying on of hands to impart the Holy Spirit. The writings of the Church Fathers of the early centuries give us much testimony of the celebration of initiation of newcomers into the community. This initiation became very elaborate. First the candidate was baptized, then he was led to the bishop who confirmed the baptism or entrance into the community by imposition of hands or anointing, and finally the newly baptized was conducted to his first full participation in the Eucharist. In these early ages there seems to have been no conception of a separate sacrament of confirmation, but there was frequent reference to the anointing as a "sealing with the Holy Spirit."

When confirmation came to be considered as a separate sacrament in the Middle Ages, some further explanations emerged. Though the history of the theological explanations is very intricate and involves a good deal of technical language, the central idea which emerges can be presented very simply. Confirmation, like baptism, is seen as a sacrament that confers a "character" or mark on the person, giving him a role in the Church, that is, in the task of the redemption of the world. The patristic references to the "sealing" with the Spirit were understood as stamping a mark or badge on the candidate which designates him for a public office.

It was often said that the particular public office was the celebration of the Eucharist. In answer to the question as to what, then, constitutes the difference between the mark or badge of the baptized person and that of the confirmed, several answers have been offered. It has been said that confirmation is the sacrament of Christian maturity. Obviously, people do not attain moral or spiritual maturity suddenly, but only very gradually in the course of their lives. Therefore, it is important to understand what kind of maturity is at stake here.

Another explanation makes it clearer by saying that baptism makes a person a Christian in a more or less passive sense and confirmation does so in an active sense. This goes back to a very old traditional theme which connects baptism with Easter and confirmation with Pentecost. At Easter the Apostles experienced in a vivid way the resurrection of Jesus from his terrible death. They knew then that Jesus had brought redemption into the world and that they had received that redemption, and they believed in him. It is only when we read the Pentecost story that we are told the other half of their response. In the power of the Spirit of God they then realize that they must organize themselves into a community of believers, the Church, so as to bring salvation to others.

The traditional order of initiation suggests that a person is first baptized into the death and resurrection of Christ, believing in Jesus as his savior and entering the community of believers. He is then confirmed in the Church as one who assumes the responsibility of actively making salvation by Jesus accessible to others. After this he is ready to assemble with other Christians to offer the Eucharist, because the Eucharist is the central action that constitutes the Church.

This is why people who have studied the history and the theory of the liturgy always insist that the sacrament of confirmation should come before the first reception of Holy Communion. However, they are also concerned that it is much more appropriate that the Bishop be the one to confirm, because it is appropriate that the bishop be the one to provide the badge for public service in the Church. For practical reasons, our insistence on confirmation by the Bishop has in the recent past usually meant that most children received Communion before their confirmation simply because the Bishop did not come to each parish that often.

Those who have been concerned with pastoral theology and practice in the context of education, action, or psychology have been pleading for a much later age for confirmation. They have suggested that since baptism has not been a personal choice for most Christians

Confirmation and the personal dimension   27

today and since personal choice is quite essential to the task of being a Christian, we really need a moment of personal choice that can be publicly celebrated. Confirmation seems to offer just this. If it is the sacrament of maturity as a Christian, the sacrament of active assumption of Church membership and apostolic responsibilities, then there is much to be said for waiting until the candidate is both ready and truly willing to make a fully adult commitment.That would be in his late teens or early twenties and sometimes much later.

At first sight, this seems like an insoluble dilemma. Liturgically, it is advisable to have confirmation before First Communion, but psychologically and pastorally it is advisable to have it in young adulthood. The problem, however, is not entirely insoluble. No one wants to exclude young people and children from the Eucharist. It is by their sharing in the worship of the community that some enthusiasm and understanding for the task of being a Christian can be passed on. The liturgy, furthermore, is the best way of learning really to pray. Yet it is quite possible that the Solemn Communion need not be the first one.

A child is indeed a passive Christian. He does what he sees other people doing and often does not realize the implications of it at all. There is no reason he could not participate and receive Communion along with his parents and as part of their celebration of the Eucharist, even though he cannot possibly understand what it means to associate oneself with the death and resurrection of Jesus in the expectation of his coming again.

There is really no good reason he cannot just "tag along" with his parents until one day much, much later when he has declared that he wants to be a fully active, responsible adult member, and has been confirmed as such. Then he could be conducted into the Church for the Eucharist and celebrate his solemn communion with the public celebration of the whole parish. At this time his Solemn Communion would mean that he is more than a receiver of this Eucharist but is uniting himself to the death and resurrection of Christ, so as to help constitute the reality of the Church for the salvation of others.

Such a plan, of course, implies great respect for the freedom and conscience of the adolescent. There comes a time when a child can no longer do things just because his parents are doing them, but he is by no means ready yet to make his own adult decisions and commitments. At this time it is important that there be adult persons outside his family whom he admires and to whom he can turn with full confidence that they are worthy of imitation and trust and that they will not try to force him or overwhelm him into making the commitment they have made. A live parish should be full of such people providing a living demonstration of what life and Church and adult responsibility really are.

There is no way of respecting someone's freedom while still guaranteeing ahead of time the choices he will make with that freedom. For many people there is a long "religious latency" period, that is, a span of years in which the individual's total attention is so actively engaged in more concrete and immediate objectives that he experiences religious questions and commitments as not "relevant" to his life and purpose. To coax or bully him to go on with it anyway, as an irrelevant activity that makes him more acceptable to the community, is not helpful and runs the risk of making it impossible for him to discover later that it is fundamentally and quite essentially relevant to his life.

At this point many people have questions about grace

and the salvation of the individual concerned. People will sometimes suggest that children should receive the sacraments of initiation as early as possible and should be herded to Confession and Communion without consulting their wishes, because they do not know what is good for them, and meanwhile we make sure that they receive a lot of grace to give them strength against the turbulence of adolescence and the temptations of life.

This may rest on an inadequate understanding of grace. Grace is not a substance, or a sort of electric charge that can be poured in and stored independently of the personal growth and development of the person. Grace is basically a personal relationship to God, the friendship of God offered to us. God does not ration out his friendship, as though one would have to participate in the Eucharist many, many times before he really becomes generous, or as though one would have to go to Confession very frequently before he decides really to give the grace to overcome sin and sinfulness. The only reason for repeating participation in the sacraments lies in ourselves and our gradual growth and development. God offers the totality of His friendship at all times and in any one sacramental celebration. The reason we have many different celebrations is that they are supposed to be signs to us to bring home to us the presence and efficacy of God's grace in the different circumstances of our lives.

This means that a child who has been baptized has already been offered the fullness of God's friendship. God does not withhold His Spirit or the fulness of His gifts of grace until confirmation. The person receives the gift of the Spirit as and when he is mature and ready and fully open to it. The sacrament of confirmation is supposed to bring him to this personal readiness with the help of the full cooperation of the community of believers. It will be most apt to do this if it is given at the most appropriate moment in the development of the individual, as far as the community or its leaders can judge. It will be least apt to do this if given long, long before the person has the human faculties to understand what is happening, and without a careful drawing out of the implications later.

Some people also raise the question of salvation of the individual if he is given so much freedom in adolescence that he may wander off altogether and never return to a regular churchgoing Christian commitment. This raises the question of the relation between Church and salvation. It is quite clear in the tradition of the Church and has been made fully explicit in the teaching of Vatican II, that an individual need not be a confessing member of the visible Church to be saved, but that the Church is necessary in the world so that mankind may be saved. In other words, the vocation of being a Christian is the task of helping Jesus knowingly in the salvation of the world in the way that he has pointed out. This, of course, is a most fruitful way of salvation for the individual himself but it is not the only way an individual can be saved. Therefore, it is most important to offer Church membership in the fullest sense to everyone, but not to attempt to force it on anyone who is not ready to make the commitment of his own free will.

Some Catholics may look back rather regretfully on their own confirmation, thinking that it had very little meaning for them at the time, and some parents and teachers may be worried, knowing that they are preparing children for confirmation when these children are too young to have an inkling of what an adult Christian commitment might mean, simply because it is required by the custom of the parish or diocese. The fact that the sacrament has been celebrated before it had a meaning does not prevent anyone from personally appropriating the meaning later on, if and when it begins to dawn on him.

This is probably why "baptism of the Spirit" is now frequently heard of among Catholics. It is the personal and public celebration of the confirmation that did not have its full meaning for them when it was received. Not everyone can point to one overwhelming moment when he recognized the outpouring of the Spirit on him and opened himself to it. For some people this can come very slowly and almost imperceptibly, but later if they reflect on it they realize that the gift of the Spirit has become an everyday power in their lives, shaping what they do and say and are, even though it was not so at the time of their confirmation.

Notes for Chapter II

The questions concerning nature and grace are touched very lightly in this chapter because they have been discussed in Chapter VI of the author's earlier book, *What Are the Theologians Saying?*

The most readily available full-length study of confirmation which covers the history and the theological and practical questions about the sacrament is Marian Bohen, *The Mystery of Confirmation,* published by Herder & Herder.

A careful description of the Catholic Pentecostal Movement, including autobiographical accounts of the experiences of some of its participants, is available in Kevin and Dorothy Ranaghan, *Catholic Pentecostals,* published by the Paulist Press in Deus Books.

The Breaking of bread and the celebration of liberation and peace

3

It will be evident from the foregoing chapters that the celebration of the Eucharist has been seen by Catholics through the centuries as the central action of Christians and the core of the Church. It may not be equally evident why. Most of us are aware that, practically speaking in our times, the Sunday Mass obligation is what seems to hold the Catholic community together and give it some continuity, definition and identification. We are equally aware that this view has both advantages and disadvantages. It guarantees the presence of large numbers of people where they can be influenced, even if they are only minimally committed. It also means, however, that we seldom have a Eucharistic celebration in which the whole congregation fully participates and everyone really wants to be there.

Until very recently this state of affairs was simply taken for granted among Catholics, at least in the English-speaking countries. Today this is no longer so. People are asking, "Why should I go to Mass on Sundays if it is not relevant to my life, if the liturgy is dull and unimaginative and poorly performed, if the sermon is out of date and unconnected with life and intolerably boring, if I can pray better at home or if I can make my work my prayer?" To answer these questions honestly and adequately requires far more than a liturgical understanding of the Eucharist. To solve the problem honestly requires far more than an updating of the rubrics and texts and an improvement of the style of celebration. What is required is a living understanding of the way the Eucharist grows out of a far-reaching commitment of one's everyday life, as well as a desire to participate in the Eucharist as the community's effort to join forces in renewing and deepening that commitment by a meeting of minds and a joining of purpose with Jesus Christ.

To understand what is at stake, it is helpful to retrace the biblical theme of liberation from Exodus to the Paschal Mystery and to observe its celebration in the Passover *seder*, including that of the Last Supper. It will also be helpful to consider some aspects of traditional Christian Eucharistic spirituality, which are much broader in their implications than might be evident from casual acquaintance with Catholic doctrinal definitions of the theology of the Eucharist.

The biblical theme of liberation is not as concrete or as simple in its images and stories as the baptismal theme of rebirth from water or the confirmation theme of quickening by the breath of God. When John the Evangelist looks for a similar concrete image to sum up the liberation theme, he uses that of blood, though scripture and tradition also give equal weight to the theme of bread. To understand the interweaving of these two symbols in the theme of liberation it is necessary to try to live and relive the reality of Exodus personally.

In the Passover *seder* celebration, Israel recalls the days of its enslavement and distress in Egypt. It is not enough that the ancestors were delivered by the power of God. Each generation must experience the liberation in its own life experience. Therefore, each generation must enter into the bitter experience of slavery, of being held in contempt, of deep alienation and the sense of rejection, of feeling that there is no escape from the vicious circle of violence and fear and hate, of not knowing whether life is worth living at all. Without really experiencing this, it is not possible to understand what the liberation of Exodus means. The meaning cannot be conveyed simply by an explanation in words, but only by an experience.

There seem to be three levels of interpretation of an event or person or a commitment. The first and basic way to interpret a piece of music (that is, to understand it) is to be able to play it. The basic way to interpret a prayer is to be able to pray it and really mean it and allow one's life and values to be shaped by it. The basic way to interpret or understand a liberating event is personally to live through it and allow it to reverberate in one's feelings and thoughts and actions.

A second way to interpret or understand a piece of music would be to listen to it in imagination without actually playing it or hearing it played. If I do not have the instruments, that may be my only access to the music. A second way of interpreting or understanding a prayer is to watch or imagine the life and experience of the one who prays it. If my own life is not sufficiently focussed or my own experience is not sufficiently mature to pray that prayer myself, then the attempt to enter into the life of another by imagination, by empathy, may be my only access to the prayer in

The breaking of bread   35 its true meaning—even, for instance, with the Lord's Prayer. A second way to understand a liberating event is likewise to imagine the experience of those who undergo it, to try to empathize in every dimension of one's own life experience with what happened to those who have been through the liberating experience. This second level of interpretation or understanding is the principle of all religious celebration. It is the principle on which the *seder* is built for the Jews and it is the principle on which the Eucharist and all the sacraments are built for Christians.

There is a third level of interpretation or understanding. The music can be interpreted in terms of words used about it, words that classify, describe and compare with other pieces, and so on. The prayer can be explained in terms of when and how it was composed, in terms of identifying the references or allusions, explaining the vocabulary and so forth. The experience can also be analyzed and classified in this way. What is very important, however, is that such an explanation is absolutely useless to anyone who has not been able to share in the first or second kind of understanding. The personal living of the reality, or the vicarious living of the reality always tends to express itself in verbal and conceptual explanations. But when a person is given only the verbal or conceptual explanations, these will never of themselves lead him to the experience. This is why scripture speaks very little in abstract or systematic formulations. It gives us a rather untidy collection of stories, experiences, reflections, prayers, complaints and other presentations which invite our reliving of someone else's experience in order to deepen and broaden our own.

About alienation and misery and unfreedom we are told the story of Israel in Egypt. The first six chapters of the book of Exodus describe a bitter enslavement. The Egyptians oppress the Hebrews in such a way that there seems no possible way out of it all. Any step one of them could take towards freedom would have such terrible consequences for the others that none dares do such a thing. As a price of freedom, some men must make great sacrifices on behalf of the people, for instance, the overseers in the public works program. But the account that we are given suggests not only enslavement by the Egyptians, but a slave mentality. The Hebrews do not believe that they can be free, that they can ever be masters of their own destiny, that they can ever live as men rather than as chattels and servants of other men. They are therefore not prepared to make any sacrifices for their own freedom—much less for the freedom of others. They are not prepared for extra effort, for great self-discipline, for the task of building a community, working towards a common goal. The only thing they seem to have in common is their alienation, their bitter suffering and oppression. Their experience is one of total and inescapable powerlessness.

Into the midst of this comes a very sharp, challenging summons from God to Moses to set the people free. God, as He appears in Exodus 33, is supremely free. One can never quite grasp Him. He is not seen. Even His name is elusive. He is not bound to any particular place or time. He does not accept the limits and impossibilities that are so obvious in the situation. He always seems to call out of a future that does not yet exist, and to talk about things and situations that do not yet exist as though they were actualities. He commands the impossible and it becomes possible by His command. What is interesting above all is the passionate way God concerns Himself with the freedom of men really to live as men. His concern is concrete, political, economic, social, personal and communal.

How God is known and how His intervention in history becomes evident is described for us in very colorful language in Exodus 33. The people indeed think that God talks to Moses face to face as one man talks with another, but the subsequent story suggests that it is not exactly like that. Moses yearns for a more tangible presence of God, for clear instructions, for a vision that would let him know he is not just imagining it all. But he is told that man cannot see the face of God and live. He will see the splendor of God pass by showing favor to people who have in no way earned it and pouring out compassion on those who have not particularly deserved it, liberating them out of hopeless situations apparently in spite of themselves. And when the impossible has happened, Moses will be able to look back and reflect and know that God has been there. He will see God, so to speak, from the back.

The Bible presents Moses as a great mystic, living with a kind of courage and clarity of vision that most of us never attain. Most of us and most of Israel have not been very ready to expose ourselves in faith to the full force of experience in our own lives and in the lives of our people. Neither have we been too well disposed to reflect on past events in the light of faith to allow the liberating power of God's intervention to reverberate in our lives. As a matter of fact, most of us during most of our lives do not even make enough leisure time for ourselves to reflect in this lofty fashion. Our time, effort and attention are almost always focussed on immediate and individual goals—raising our children; buying, repairing, decorating and maintaining our homes; trying to keep our jobs or win promotion; planning vacations, trips, material additions and improvements; trying to get enough money to buy the things that we have set our hearts on.

In the midst of this everyday life we might very well not see people around us and in our world today who are as unfree as the Hebrews in Egypt. We might not realize the ways that we ourselves are unfree and contribute to the unfreedom of others. We might simply be too busy to notice. Our vision might just be too sharply focussed on our individual, or family, or local or national wants to hear the sort of thing that Moses heard. This is why both Israel and Christian tradition have found it necessary to provide a community support for this kind of reflection in which God reveals Himself.

In the *seder* the families of the people of Israel have gathered .year after year through the centuries and through the millennia to enter into the experience of Exodus in a ritual celebration. As they set a table and prepare a meal according to the prescriptions with the unleavened bread, the shank bone of the lamb, the wine, the bitter herbs, the egg, and the dish that represents the mortar, they realize that what they are entering into is a multi-dimensional meditation. It is a deeply personal experience and it is a communal experience of all Israel.

The participants know that the feast has at least three names. It is *Pesach* or Passover, because the vengeance of God passed over and spared the firstborn of the Hebrews when the firstborn of the Egyptians were slain. It is also the "feast of the unleavened bread" which is understood to mean the "bread of affliction." Finally, it is "the time of our freedom."

There is some very deep thought contained in the explanation of unleavened bread as the bread of affliction. Leaven is symbolic of wickedness, because that is how evil spreads—like a hidden leaven working its way through the whole dough. Before the celebration of Passover begins, Jewish tradition prescribes that there is to be a hunt through the house to make sure that all leaven and anything that has leaven in it (like beer and cake and bread) is to be destroyed or removed from the house. The Bible tells us that when Israel left Egypt they baked unleavened bread in their haste; it was the bread of affliction. But it was out of their affliction and through their affliction that God called them into freedom, into the utterly new life that broke the vicious circle of the inescapable consequences of evil deeds. Bread was leavened traditionally by using some sour dough from a previous batch. If you want to begin afresh and absolutely free from some contamination from the past, you have to begin with unleavened bread, and the unleavened bread will be the bread of affliction, of passing through a bitter suffering or a kind of death.

Passover is the "time of our freedom." This means more than the once-for-all freedom from the slavery of Egypt in times of old. It means the freedom that must be won and paid for now, this year, in the lifetime of this generation. It means the freedom of mankind that is yet in the future. Exodus, the going out from the slavery of Egypt, becomes the paradigm for a liberation from all kinds of enslavement and all kinds of alienation—liberation from enslavement to petty wants and attachments; liberation from all kinds of racism, partisan and exclusive positions; liberation from want and fear and war and despair; liberation from boredom with life and from depression.

Israel sees only one way of real and final freedom and that is the way towards a total and unreserved engagement with God. For Israel, God is freedom and

God's law is nothing different from the demands of genuine human freedom, the conditions for realizing authentic and universal human freedom. When Israel celebrates Passover, the families try to enter into the great Exodus event so that it is no longer then but becomes now, and when it becomes here and now, they ask themselves what it demands of them here and now, this year, to bring about the reign of God in the world and to move towards the promised freedom for all men.

Jesus preached about the reign of God and he preached about setting men free, and even his closest friends and followers seem to have had considerable difficulty understanding what he was talking about. He himself knew that he could not tell them in words. He could only communicate the meaning of freedom by the life that he lived among them and particularly by the way he would bring his life to its conclusion in death. Only in his death would they be able to glimpse the startling authenticity of his freedom and be able to see it in terms of his total and unreserved engagement with the Father.

Jesus had celebrated Passover many times but Matthew's gospel tells us that he looked forward to his final *seder* celebration with passionate desire because it would mark the coming of the reign of God (Lk. 22, 15-16). This was a special celebration. In it Jesus entered with his disciples into the Exodus experience as usual and asked as usual what the task of liberation or redemption of mankind demanded here and now of this household this year. And looking into the celebration as the experience in which the Father reveals Himself, Jesus reads in it the answer which is the mystery of his own death. And still the disciples who are gathered there do not understand. We know from their questions as reported in John 13 and 14 that they do not understand, and that Jesus will have to sustain the hope and vision and make the sacrifice that is the price of freedom for mankind, quite alone and without their support. The subsequent recital of the agony in the garden gives us some vague glimpse of the total experience of abandonment and rejection and failure of the mission that results from the fact that even they even now do not understand.

At the *seder*, then, in the course of the usual ritual actions and explanations, Jesus takes the unleavened bread which is the bread of affliction out of which the totally new life of freedom comes and he meditates aloud with and for his disciples. This bread is his body, because his body is to be broken and given for the redemption, the liberation of the world. His death is to be the bread of affliction to sustain new life.

Bread has so many levels of meaning. It is the gift of God, but a gift that must be received with toil and patience. Man must till and sow and wait for sun and rain and harvest time. The grain will grow but man must reap and thresh and grind and knead and bake. It is in his own labor that he recognizes and receives the gift of God. In Hebrew tradition the blessing or praise of God at meals is said in the breaking of bread which draws the family together in recognition of God's gift of life. In the Passover *seder* this acquires another level of meaning when the bread of affliction is broken for the life and community of the whole people in the gift of God. In Jesus' *seder* celebration there is a level of meaning in the breaking of the bread that is so deep that one might well become dizzy and terrified looking down into it. That is why we do it with all the support of a community celebration in which people sustain one another by their shared commitment.

Again in the course of the prescribed ceremonies,

Jesus takes the last cup of blessing and meditates aloud with them. The meal is over and it is the time of the singing of the *Hallel,* the great Psalms of praise. This cup of wine, Jesus says, is the cup of his blood which is to be shed for those present and for many for forgiveness and reconciliation and redemption.

Wine also has many levels of meaning. It is a rather special gift of God because of its quality of intoxication. It also is produced only by considerable human labor and ingenuity. We have wine because grapes are trampled on and crushed. The theme that men are like grapes growing on the vine often appears in the Bible. Israel as a whole is like a vine planted by God to give a wine of joy. The poor of God, the humble men of faith whose lives are fully engaged to God and to the coming of His reign, are like grapes. Out of their oppression and distress comes joy.

Wine is the blood of the grape. It is the life of the plant just as blood is the life of man. Extraction of the juice of the grape is its death, and the shedding of blood is the death of man. Redemption or freedom is obtained at the price of death or willingness to die. Blood was the symbol of Exodus when it was smeared on the doorposts in Egypt (Exodus 12,7) and when it was sprinkled over the people in the desert in token of their commitment to the covenant with God (Exodus 24,7-8). Jesus makes his own blood the symbol of our entrance into the great covenant with God, and links it with the blood of the grape that is used in Passover and the Eucharist.

In these great moments of symbolic action, Jesus reaches out to those present and to those of us who would subsequently call ourselves his followers. He offers us his presence and his life—the extension of his body through time and space making himself acces-

The breaking of bread   43

sible to us in the celebration of this action, and the pouring out of his blood by emptying himself of individual claims in order to be entirely for others, for us. And as he does this, he leaves his instructions that, after he is gone and we begin to understand and rally to his mission in the world, we should gather to celebrate this event again and again. Each time we celebrate we are to try to reach out to him as he reaches out to us. We are to try to enter into the experience of his death and its meaning to him and to us, trying to broaden our vision to the dimensions of his vision, to raise our goals in life to the height of his goals, and to overcome the alienation and unfreedom and confusion of our lives by bringing them into confrontation with the utter freedom and simplicity of his engagement with the Father.

Through the ages the Christian community has tried to do this. Its celebration of Eucharist has been its attempt to constitute itself the community of the followers of Jesus. The Eucharist has been seen both as the source of Christian life and action in the world, and as the outcome of it. There is a sense in which the Christian task of redemption is something to which each follower of Jesus responds in utter solitude and in a unique way. There is also a sense in which we must show one another the face of God, making the reality of God's presence and action in the world tangible.

This is the subject matter of the following chapter, which will take up some aspects of Christian Eucharistic spirituality and discuss the relationship of public worship and private prayer, of communal and personal commitment. It will be only after this discussion that there can be any sensible answer to the question, "Why should I go to Mass on Sundays?"

Notes to Chapter III

The topic of "real presence" has not been discussed at the level of systematic explanation for two reasons. It is so discussed in Chapter IV of the author's earlier book, *What Are the Theologians Saying?* Moreover, it would seem that most people who are not theologians are not spontaneously interested in the question unless theologians and catechists set out to make it a problem for them.

For the understanding of "interpretation" used in this chapter and elsewhere in this book, the author is indebted to lectures of the philosopher Hans Georg Gadamer and to the *Spiritual Exercises of St. Ignatius.*

The Hebrew background to the Eucharist is given very simply and very adequately in a small book by Isaac Levy, *Guide to Passover,* written for Jews. It is published by Jewish Chronicle Publications in London, but is available through the Commentary Library in New York. Also very helpful is the booklet of the *Passover Haggadah* which is available with English translation from Shulsinger Brothers Press in New York and as a Schocken Press paperback.

A brief and comprehensive account of the various aspects of the Eucharist for Christians is available by Bernard Cooke, *The Eucharist, Mystery of Friendship* in the Pflaum/Standard Witness Books. Also helpful is Charles Davis, *Liturgy & Doctrine,* published by Sheed & Ward.

Church, prayer and Sunday 4

It seems at first contradictory to say that the Mass
matters most to those Christians who are most radically
secular in their commitment. It is, however, true. We
are considerably hampered today in understanding
what the action of the Eucharist is, because it is easier
to see a certain "churchiness" in our worship and lives,
than to see the commitment that is involved in being
a Christian in the world.

One might get the superficial impression that six
days a week have to be devoted to our own and our
family interests, but that we set aside a little time on
Sunday which, unlike the rest of the week, is devoted
to God and therefore is a good investment for salvation.
Similarly, one might have the impression that our cities
are built and organized for immediate practical interests of a social, economic and political nature, but that
there are some buildings and some organizations,
churches, that are intended not for practical purposes
of living together in the world but for the quite different

purpose of relating men to God. Finally, one might also think that a man's activities have to be realistically concerned with making his way in the world and protecting his interests against other people and worrying about the here and now, but that a little sector of his life should be taken up with prayer, which is a very different sort of concern.

The Bible and Christian tradition give us a different understanding of reality from this. The sacred and the secular are not two different sectors of life, or two different areas in space and time; they are two different ways of seeing and responding to the whole of reality. In the burning bush story in Exodus 3, Moses is told to take off his shoes because the ground on which he stands is holy. But it turns out that that does not mean the particular spot of earth, because God is not tied to any one place. It means that any ground is holy, because God is everywhere—not only in places officially designated for worship but in homes, streets, offices, factories.

But the story suggests we have a problem in recognizing the holiness. Somehow, sometime, some place, we have to make the effort to take our shoes off and be open to the experience of holiness. Although all sectors of life are the expression of God's presence and power and concern, it seems that most of us, most of the time, find it far more obvious to see reality exclusively in terms of our control over things. It is more customary for us to experience life and reality as something we seize and hold onto by our own efforts rather than as something that is a gift held out to us.

Often people say, "I've worked for everything I've got. I deserve to be where I am and enjoy the fruits of my labor. If other people are poor, why don't they work harder? You've got to look out for yourself. If you don't, nobody will. If everybody just minded his own business and worked his own way up, the world would be a better place." Or people might say, "The priests shouldn't meddle in social and political matters. Let them preach about religion and get us to heaven and stop worrying about race and war and poverty, which are matters of this world." Again, people are inclined to say, "Politics is politics and business is business. Business is run to make the most profit for the people who have the power to make others work for them. It can have no other objectives. A government works for the advantage of its own country or of those within it who can keep the government in power. It cannot concern itself with the common good of nations; the latter has to emerge as best it can from the power struggle. Wars, injustice, poverty and oppression are inevitable. Anyone who thinks we can end them is unrealistic."

Such notions as these are startling but typical examples of secularistic thinking. They are the opposite of faith. The man of faith knows that all that he has is a gift that he could never really have deserved, and that he can never judge others but only try to share his good fortune with them. The man of faith knows that all human experience is the realm of sin and redemption and that this includes war and poverty and race. The man of faith knows that the world can be redeemed, that the consequences of evil deeds are not forever inescapable, that the world is not inevitably headed for nuclear holocaust and disaster. But in terms of everyday experience looked at without faith, the man of faith is an irresponsible optimist.

Many people told Moses he was an irresponsible optimist. They insisted that the slavery in Egypt was something that could not possibly be ended and they gave good logical demonstrations for this. Many people told Jesus he was an unrealistic dreamer. He spoke of the reign of God being possible now, if only people would believe in him and live that way. He was told that it was an absurd suggestion while the Roman occupation was in force, but he refused to join the Zealots, the resistance movement. He was told that anyone with any common sense could see that, under the circumstances, there had to be a separation of religious goals from the realms of politics and economics and social structure, but he refused to follow the priestly party in its accommodation to injustice. He maintained against all the evidence that the reign of God could be now and is hidden in the hearts of men waiting to become a visible reality in the redemption of the world from injustice and fear and despair.

The death of Jesus seemed to many people to confirm the fact that he was quite mistaken about the possibility of the reign of God becoming an accomplished fact then. Even the apostles had to work their way through a terrible despair. But what is significant is that some people saw the Risen Jesus with the greatest clarity, and others looked at exactly the same evidence but they could not see the Resurrection. It seems to happen at all times of history and in all sorts of situations that some people are able to look at the events that have happened and reflect on them and see the wonderful works of God and others are not able to see anything more than a disaster or a depressing and inescapable situation. Even the most obvious miracle could never change this, because such people can find a way to explain it by an extension of the present scientific and technological theories.

What seems to be at stake is a person's expectation, which is built on what he is doing with his life. One can look at the world as though there were no freedom of God or men. Then he will calculate the chances of future events statistically as in a laboratory experiment. In that case nothing really new can ever happen. We are trapped forever into the consequences of evil deeds. That is secularistic thinking.

However, one can also look at the world expecting freedom and expecting God's promise and salvation to break in. Then he will ask what he can do, and consider the past and present not statistically but for its hints of a possible breakthrough to a new liberation. It is, of course, quite possible that a man may delude himself into supposing he has more freedom than is actually the case, but events will show him his limits. On the other hand, a man never has any more freedom than he thinks he has. When we assume that we are unfree to remedy a situation, then we really are unfree until someone redeems us.

We are all unfree in many ways. There are people with whom we cannot get along. There are events of which we are afraid, especially death—our own and that of others. The freedom and unpredictability of others tends to threaten us. We are often caught in uncomfortable situations where we are playing out an unauthentic role and somehow feel we cannot be authentic because we have to keep up appearances. We see great possibilities for the future but dare not take the risk. We have the possibility of a deep friendship but cannot bring ourselves to be so vulnerable and exposed. We got off "on the wrong foot" with someone, or in some job or in some situation, and seem forever doomed to the consequences of a misunderstanding or failure to relate. We find ourselves part of the structure of an unjust world but we realize we would be trampled if we stepped out of line. In these and many other ways, everyone does need to be redeemed.

Church, prayer and Sunday   51

Where is the freedom to come from? How can there be redemption if God calls always but it is almost impossible to hear, if God is everywhere but it is almost impossible to see, if God expresses Himself in everything but it is almost impossible to feel? The biblical answer to this is that each person must achieve a sort of quiet focus, gathering all his attention to the deepest level of his being and beyond. He must patiently and perseveringly keep looking to where reality fades into the mystery of darkness, listening until he begins to hear the silence, and opening himself so totally that he comes to feel the terrible absence of God—because the other name of darkness, silence, absence is holiness or transcendence. God, who is utter freedom, is known in the demands that He makes on our freedom. He is known as redeemer, liberator, as He who calls out of chaos and misery and alienation to purposefulness and freedom and meaning in life.

But the biblical answer has another facet. This apparently impossible task becomes possible through a community and a tradition that sustains it. To pray in utter silence without words or images or actions is terrifying and men cannot sustain it. This fearful encounter with silence becomes possible only when we build a language of prayer together and help one another to look and listen and feel as God reveals Himself.

No one has ever seen God directly, nor heard nor felt His presence. As Christians, we expect the self-revelation of the Father when we look at the face of Jesus, listen to his voice and feel for his presence. But Jesus is no longer directly accessible to our looking, listening and feeling either. He is accessible as communicated by his followers, no more and no less.

The words that we can hear are those that his dis-

chapter four

ciples heard and recalled and recorded. If we hear them only as read from the book that was written long ago, they will sound stale and flat and strange. If we hear them spoken straight out of the lived experience of Christians today, the words will be the living words of the living Christ. The face that we see has the features that were seen and observed and described by his disciples. If we hear only mechanical repetitions of those descriptions it will mean very little, but once we have recognized those features in those whose lives have really been assimilated to that of Jesus we are unlikely ever again to forget the face.

The redeeming, liberating presence of Jesus can be communicated only by a liberating presence of those who have in their turn been redeemed by him. If we who are the Church only talk about that presence instead of personally being that presence to others inside and outside Church circles, our talking will not make much sense to anyone.

This is what we try to do as Church. We who have been reborn into the life of the Risen Jesus and who have caught the breath of the Spirit try to be the saving presence of Jesus in the world. This is in a basic sense a worldly or secular (not secularistic) task. It means supporting one another and banding together to change the quality of human life from despair to hope, from an all-pervasive fear and suspicion to trust, from war to peace, from heedless competition to co-operation, from anxiety to joy, from shallow drifting to purposeful integration, from oppression of the poor and weak to justice for all. This is what Jesus said he had come to do, when he quoted the passage from Isaiah in his home town synagogue (Luke 4,16-22).

For this, each Christian must certainly enter in great personal depth into the prayer of Jesus himself, to attain a steadiness of purpose and clarity of vision that makes it possible to live like this in a world that is structured in the opposite direction. To be radically secular and concerned with the world as a Christian, a person needs to be very firmly rooted in faith. This faith is the focus towards the transcendent God, and our tradition has always said that that focus is practiced by prayer.

We have three paradigms for prayer—three ways of thinking and talking about it: a conversation with God (the listening aspect), contemplation (the looking aspect), and raising of one's spirit to God (the presence aspect). Whichever of these ways of thinking we choose, it means that the individual is very dependent on learning it from his tradition. It commonly happens that a person takes the words and actions and symbols of his tradition and repeats them until he begins to penetrate their meaning. Then he finds himself launching out into words (perhaps also gestures and symbols) of his own. But after some time he realizes that all words are inadequate and that he is talking too much and listening too little and he fades into an embarrassed silence.

It would be very tempting to give up at this point and say that praying makes no sense and that one's work is prayer or that other people are prayer. But it is very important not to give up at this point but to keep listening to the silence. People who do often find it terrifying, but sooner or later they tend to find words again, the same words of the traditional prayers of scripture and the liturgy and the tradition, and perhaps very simple words of their own. But the words have a far deeper meaning than they ever had before.

Some people say they keep circling back into silence and that each time it becomes less embarrassing but more frightening. Abraham said it was like falling into a trance (Genesis 15,12). Moses said he sometimes had occasion to doubt his own sanity (Exodus 33,12-23). Elijah said he wished he were dead (I Kings 19). Jesus said, "My God, my God, why have you forsaken me?" (Mark 15,33-36). People cannot sustain the silence of God alone.

The celebrations of the community offer the starting point and the mutual support for every Christian endeavor in action and in prayer. In the course of the ages we have set aside places that are rallying points. The church is not supposed to be the place that contains the Christian faith, as though there were no place for it outside the walls of the church building. It is supposed to be a place that sustains it by being a symbol of God's dwelling among men everywhere, and by collecting many signs and symbols that will refresh the vision and focus of those that enter the building so that they may see the world in a different perspective when they come out of it.

From the very earliest times in our tradition we set aside the Sunday, the Lord's day, for a celebration of the Eucharist in which it was assumed that the whole community would be represented. The Jewish idea of Sabbath is that it is the day of rest and reflection when men can focus their attention beyond their own petty individual concerns and try to identify with the concerns of God, the redeemer of the world. It is a day of leisure, because only in leisure can men find a deeper focus and realize the invitation to freedom. If one never gets out of the everyday routine and drudgery, it is unlikely that one will be creative about the future and imagine in any radical way that things could be different.

Christians built up an understanding of the first day

of the week as the special day of the Risen Christ by calling it the Eighth Day. The circle of time had already been broken because in the resurrection of Jesus eternity had broken in, that is to say, the reign of God had already been experienced. When Christians assembled for a weekly celebration of a "little Easter," they gathered to recall their joint involvement in making the reign of God public and evident in the transformation of the world. In the early centuries it is quite clear that they saw one means to this and that was to transform themselves into a witness community. They tried to live the reality of the reign of God among themselves.

Each gathering was a recommitment, a common meditation and an offering of mutual support. While persons were baptized into the community only once, and received the imposition of hands in petition of the Spirit only once, their Eucharistic participation was not exhausted by the initiation rites. It was repeated on every Lord's day, because the entrance into the mystery of the death and resurrection of Jesus is progressive both for the community and for each member.

Each Eucharist in a sense recapitulates initiation because it includes an entrance rite, reading, instruction and meditation of scripture, and a profession of faith, leading into the Eucharistic celebration. But the heart of it is the reenactment of the gestures and words of Jesus in the effort of the community to be fully present to meet the presence of Jesus that he extends to them in this gesture—fully present to try to see with his eyes and reach out with his effort. In this, the whole symbol-language of words and actions and things used makes the meeting possible. But it would be a great mistake to suppose that this happens by itself without the active participation of the members of the gathering. They determine whether that symbol-language is

chapter four

alive or dead. They determine whether it communicates and whether a meeting is possible.

The Eucharistic gathering and its symbol-language has acquired a classic shape, though we have adapted it extensively for different times and places and different kinds of gatherings. The reason for the classic shape is that this community gathering must offer the starting point for the personal prayer of many people at different levels of maturity and different stages of penetration into the mystery of the death and resurrection of Jesus as the opening of the reign of God. It must give support to those who are just beginning to acquire a language of prayer, and to those who have launched out into their own words, and to those who are in a phase of silence and to those who have returned to words with great simplicity.

The meaning of the celebration is far more than the conceptual meaning of the words used. It carries a very extensive aura of implications and connotations. For some people what is most important is the atmosphere of recollection and worship. For others the words of scripture invoke many themes and stories around which they have structured the meaning of their lives. For some the sense of common commitment is a vital source of strength in a difficult life. Others may only be looking for some explicit instructions in the readings or homily that are immediately relevant to their lives. Because of the variety of participation, some people will tend to be conservative in their evaluation of liturgies and others will look for constant change.

People sometimes feel that if they cannot see any immediate application of the scripture readings that these should be dropped in favor of selections from modern authors for the sake of "relevance." The question, however, could really be asked, not why the scripture readings are not relevant to the people, but why the expectations of the people are not relevant to the task of redemption. It could be simply that we are talking too much and listening too little. Prayer is our participation in revelation. It is allowing God to reveal Himself, when we are open and receptive to the revelation. If we demand that it be relevant to our existing expectations and understanding, we also have to ask whether we are prepared to see our horizons break and to stretch to the stature of those who prayed and reflected before us.

When people ask why they should go to Mass when they can pray better at home or when they can make their work or their encounter with other people their prayer, there are many possible answers. Sometimes some people have had such bad experiences at Sunday Mass that they need a respite. But generally it is unlikely that an individual will sustain the frightening encounter with the silence of God, without the support of a community that shares its commitment and its worship. An individual who can sustain it will probably want to participate in the community celebration because he will feel a strong commitment to build up the community and support others. Moreover, Jesus most particularly offered this as the place of encounter with him. Yet it must be said that any real encounter or commitment must be built on more than fear of breaking a law, and that the strongest celebrations are those where everyone really wants to be present.

Notes for Chapter IV
The basic ideas of the Church in this chapter are drawn largely from three documents of Vatican II, *Lumen Gentium* (Dogmatic Constitution on the

Church), *Gaudium et Spes* (Constitution on the Church in the Modern World) and *Sacrosanctum Concilium* (Dogmatic Constitution on the Sacred Liturgy), all available in *Documents of Vatican II*, edited by Walter Abbott and published by America Press.

The understanding of prayer follows closely that of Karl Rahner in the essay *On Prayer* published by Paulist Press in Deus Books.

The concepts of sacred space and time as related to Christian experience are discussed by Louis Bouyer in *Rite and Man* (Chapters 9 and 10), published by the University of Notre Dame Press.

The theme of Sabbath and Sunday are set out in detail by Jean Danielou in *Bible and Liturgy* (Chapters 14, 15 and 16) also published by the University of Notre Dame Press. The same theme is attractively described in a Jewish context by A. J. Heschel in *The Earth is the Lord's* and *The Sabbath,* two essays published together in one volume by Harper Torchbooks.

Also very helpful in connection with the ideas covered in this chapter is *The Desert and the City* by Thomas Gannon and George Traub, published by Macmillan.

Priesthood and ministries 5

Most Catholics are aware that Protestants have a different understanding of priesthood and of church ministries from that on which the present Catholic practice is based. They are also aware of much current discussion of the priesthood of the laity, and of questions that have been raised about the role and powers and personal lives of ordained priests. In fact, many Catholics find the discussions rather disturbing and perhaps scandalizing. They are surprised to discover that the questions that are troubling us now have been raised since the earliest days of the Church.

The earliest Christians made the claim that there is only one priesthood forever and that is the priesthood of Jesus Christ, in which his followers share. The letter to the Hebrews describes rather vividly what that priesthood of Jesus Christ means, especially in Hebrews 4,14—5,10. Priesthood here is mediation or reconciliation of men with the Father. It is accomplished by sacrifice, not a sacrifice of animals or things but the offering of one's own life and death. Jesus achieves the reconciliation by going all the way down into the arena where the real conflict between chaos and God takes place. He reflects the unchanging love of God into the world in the face of every kind of hatred, contempt, anger and rejection, and in the face of death itself.

John the Evangelist says that this presence of Jesus as the expression of God's welcome and compassionate concern was so luminous that the darkness could not smother it. Not even the darkness of death, not even the horror of a criminal execution could obscure the light that enlightens everybody born into the world. Because of this confident going into darkness, everyone can see, and because of this trusting surrender into death, everyone can live (John 1). And that is redemption. That is the sacrifice of reconciliation. That is the priesthood.

It does not consist in a ritual but in a man assuming into his experience the crushing burden of the sinfulness of the world until his life is crushed out of him for others, as the wine from grapes. This is why we reenact and celebrate the event in a ritual presentation of a cup of wine with the words, "This is my blood." But this is also why the reenactment must be as personal as the original action, in order that the ritual may have meaning. The priesthood of Jesus is authentic because he offers himself. The priestly action of the Christian community is authentic if the members personally enter into the liberating event of his death so that, in offering him, they offer themselves.

The first letter of Peter speaks of the inclusion of all the baptized, all the followers of Jesus, in his priesthood. In what was probably part of the text of a baptismal liturgy, the author describes a way of life suitable to the community of believers and anticipates that their entrance into Christ will lead them through suffering. But they will be like "stones built together into an edifice of spirit, a holy priesthood offering spiritual sacrifices acceptable to God through Jesus Christ" (I Peter 2,5). The language is rather quaint but the meaning is important. Their sharing Christ's priesthood, that is, the task of mediation and reconciliation, is closely connected with the community life they live without "anything vicious, anything deceitful, pretenses, jealousies and disparaging remarks of any kind" (I Peter 2,1). This is connected with the sharing of the priesthood because it offers spiritual sacrifices, that is, not things nor the lives of animals but the way of life of the community itself. That is the reconciliation and redemption which become possible in Jesus Christ because, in his death and resurrection, God laid the cornerstone that offers an adequate foundation for it all.

Though Christians were once no people, because they come from the scattered nations, they are being built into a people, God's people, and that makes them a royal priesthood, proclaiming by their existence and their way of life the wonderful works of God (I Peter 2,9-10). The priesthood or mediation of the Christian community is not only reconciliation for one another within the Church, but reconciliation for mankind. This is why Vatican II spoke of the Church as a seed of unity and hope for all mankind (*Lumen Gentium*, Ch. 2, No. 9). The Church tries to be that kind of community of common endeavor and mutual support and acceptance that mankind ought to be.

Because they saw the community aspect as essential to the whole task of redemption, the earliest Christians were quite conscious of the different ministries or services that contributed to the work of building up the priestly communities. They recognized charismatic gifts that enabled some to preach, teach, heal and so forth, for the building up of the whole community (I Corinthians 12) but they also recognized there were services to which people ought to be appointed because they were needed (Acts 6), like the service of organizing the distribution of community charity to those in material want.

It was clear from the beginning that there had to be some organization and, therefore, organizers had to be chosen. We do not have a clear picture of how this was done in early times, nor does the organization seem to have been the same everywhere. Some local churches seem to have been headed by a group of presbyters or elders, like a synagogue. Others were headed by a single person known as the "overseer."

One of the community-building tasks to which the Church decided, in the course of time, it ought always to make an official appointment was the task of assembling the community for the Eucharistic celebration and presiding over the celebration. Presiding in this case means playing the role of Jesus in the dramatic reenactment of the Last Supper.

The evidence that documents from the early centuries offer us suggests that the concern in officially designating men who were to preside at the Eucharist was not with "power to consecrate" in the sense of a relation to things but with the ability to celebrate and really lead the community to the encounter with Christ that constituted them Church.

Very early a pattern of bishops, priests and deacons established itself—a sort of local hierarchy which was supposed to build up and sustain the Church by its various services. In the writings of the Fathers of the

Church, there is a recurring theme that the Eucharist and the Bishop are the most important unifying factors in the community of believers, and both are expected to link the community to the Apostles' experience of the death and resurrection of Jesus.

In the early third century we have the testimony of St. Hippolytus that bishops were chosen by all the people and, if found acceptable to all the people, had hands imposed on them by other bishops while everyone prayed that the Spirit might come upon the newly chosen. We also have an account of the choosing and ordaining of presbyters and deacons, the former to help the bishop in his spiritual ministry and the latter to take charge of property and administration.

An interesting point is made in the same document, *The Apostolic Tradition*. A man who has suffered serious persecution for the faith but has survived it is not to be ordained by a laying on of hands by the bishop because he already has the office of priesthood by his confession of faith under persecution. This account is important because it shows an understanding of the role of presiding at Eucharist that involves the whole person and all his experience, not simply the correct and dignified performance of a ritual.

It is clear that Christians of that time expected the dramatic reenactment at the time of each Eucharist of the role of Jesus at the Last Supper to be reinforced by the way the presbyter lived the whole of his life. It is also clear, however, that they had similar expectations of all those whom they accepted for baptism. There is no indication in the documents we have from the patristic era that they were thinking in terms of two categories of Christians, one active (the clergy) and one passive (the laity).

Unfortunately, this division of active and passive

did come to be rather commonly accepted when Christians became the majority and Christianity came to be handed on like a cultural heritage, very often without any apparent personal conversion or commitment. In the Middle Ages the office of deacon disappeared in practice. That of bishop became a function mainly of government of Church structures. That of priest came to be focussed very sharply on the power to consecrate. Since priests were now also required to be celibate in the Western Church and were given special privileges in civil law, there emerged a separate class of "clergy." It was difficult under those circumstances to maintain an understanding of presbyterate as a ministry of facilitating the priesthood of the community—the shared single priesthood of Jesus Christ.

In modern times we are slowly beginning to rediscover and slowly trying to recapture the vitality of the early Church's understanding of ministries and offices in the community. We are beginning to realize quite clearly again that the sacrament of orders is not conferred primarily for the benefit of the one who receives it, but for the benefit of the community which needs the service to which he is being ordained.

We are also beginning to realize more clearly that there are many ministries and services that build up the Church and make it possible for the community to fulfill a priestly role in relation to the world. Some of these must by their nature be spontaneous and some may be by ordination. But this does not make one group of ministries more or less important than the other. Among those that are ordained or officially commissioned, some are for tasks that require a special charism—a free gift of God to the individual in question, which is quite obviously for the benefit of others rather than his own. That means that the choice of people for ordination to such tasks must rest upon a careful scrutiny as to whether they have this charism.

With this understanding comes the conclusion that the ministries and services that we presently cluster together under the priesthood may not always be well combined in one man, and might be better arranged into different clusters with changing culture and patterns of society. Some people ask whether everyone ordained to preside at the Eucharist needs also to be a professional theologian and prepared to administer the sacrament of penance as an official representative of the Church. Others have raised the question whether the ordained priesthood should be thought of as a full-time profession or whether it would usually be exercised better by people who also have other jobs. Many have asked whether the designation of priests by titles and special clothes is always appropriate. Today the question has arisen loudly and clearly whether it is always in the interests of the Christian community that priestly ordination should be conditional upon the acknowledgment of a personal charism of virginity.

No one can give answers to these questions by scholarship or logic. The answers really have to be created by the whole community in its effort to be a priestly people in the world. We are being told on all sides that ordained priests are facing a very serious identity crisis today, arising out of a conflict of the roles they are now expected to play with the changing patterns of the society in which they are expected to play them. It will be much easier to solve that crisis if large numbers of lay Catholics assume their active role as members of a priestly people and do not expect the ordained priests to carry the whole burden of building up the Christian community and sustaining its witness and worship alone.

Meanwhile, no matter what the answers to these questions may turn out to be, we have in our ongoing tradition a very important cluster of sacramental celebrations in which the community publicly designates its office holders and prays that the Spirit may come upon them. We have said traditionally that here, too, we are imposing a badge or mark upon the person by virtue of which he is recognized as the one who may and should play certain public roles in the community. Here too the celebration is a sign that really brings about what it signifies or stands for. It does this at many levels, not only in purely functional and organizational terms, but at every level of human experience as lived with a Christian vision and in a Christian focus.

Notes for Chapter V

It is very difficult to recommend any modern, comprehensible and systematic study on the priesthood to the non-theologian and non-ordained reader.

There is a careful historical study of the development of the priesthood in the Church of the first four centuries by James Mohler, *The Origin and Evolution of the Priesthood,* published by Alba House.

The issue of *Theological Studies* dated December 1969 has three important and not too technical essays on ministry, office and priesthood.

The best follow-up for this chapter for the lay reader might be *Lay People in the Church* by Yves Congar, published by Newman Press.

Marriage in the covenant of God and man 6

The questions that many Catholic adults have concerning marriage relate usually to indissolubility, the Church's exercise of jurisdiction over marriages, problems concerning "mixed" marriages and the promises asked of the other partner, and Church directives on birth control. Everyone of these is a real and urgent and practical question, but only marginally a theological question and only marginal to marriage itself as seen in Christian tradition. It will not be possible to solve these questions in this chapter, but it will be possible to offer a frame of reference or perspective for looking at these issues and searching for a solution.

It has been suggested that marriage became a sacrament more or less by mistake or simply by force of habit. Anthropologists have noted that people in general, primitive as well as highly civilized, like to mark with religious solemnity the more tense and challenging moments of their lives. Thus most peoples have created "rites of passage" to mark the birth of a new child into family and society, to mark the transition from childhood into adult society at puberty, to reinforce the commitment and mark the transition into a marriage and a new family, and to mark and give meaning and explanation to a death.

It would be foolish to deny that this function is indeed served in the Christian community by the sacraments of baptism, confirmation, matrimony and finally the sacraments of the sick and dying and the funeral rites. But we would also miss the point of Christian celebration if we were to explain any of the sacraments primarily in this light.

Religious commitment and its observances can have two purposes. One is to reconcile the attitudes and goals and understanding of the believer to the way things are, by giving him explanations of reality and its ultimate meaning that make it possible for him to live within his situation purposefully and happily. The other purpose is to challenge him to creative efforts to reconcile what is to what ought to be, that is to change the world in the light of a dream or a promise.

Biblical faith (Jewish and Christian) is first and foremost of the latter kind. It is concerned with transforming the world as we now have it with all the apparently inescapable consequences of evil deeds into the reign of God as we progressively glimpse the possibilities of what the reign of God might look like. Therefore, each sacramental celebration carries something of this thrust towards the realization of the apparently impossible. On the other hand, each sacramental celebration must also reconcile people's attitudes to the pain and difficulty of the struggle and the weariness of the waiting.

A formal church wedding always makes it easier for the parents of the couple to see them definitively leave home, and to realize painfully that we have all grown older and a new era has begun. It also involves the whole community, gives everybody a good excuse to get together for a grand celebration, makes it possible to assemble scattered relatives and reinforce family ties, offers the older ladies a chance for some joyful weeping and the older men the opportunity to deliver themselves of long speeches containing their philosophy of life and their favorite jokes. All of this is immensely worthwhile. But the reality that is signified and effected by a Christian celebration of a marriage goes far beyond this. As a matter of fact, marriage is not a sacrament because it is celebrated in church with religious ceremony. Rather the reverse is true. It is celebrated in church with religious ceremony because it is a sacrament.

It took twelve centuries of Christian history for our tradition to formulate a theology of marriage as a sacrament and even then we had to go on waiting to the present century for theologians to ask some of the really fundamental questions about it. There is a reason why people have had difficulty in seeing marriage as a sacrament. It is radically different from the other sacraments because it is a common human event that makes sense in a secular way in which baptism, confirmation, Eucharist and ordination do not make sense. All these are special signs that belong to Christian tradition and the ritual has to be interpreted in the tradition to be understood. Even the ceremony of marriage, the mutual self-giving of the two people, does not need any explanation as the coming through water or the imposition of hands needs explanation.

In the biblical vision of reality, marriage is a revelatory event. That is, God reveals himself when man and woman make a total commitment to each other, when they embrace in sexual union, when they become parents, when they are faithful to each other in changing circumstances, when their marriage becomes an oasis of cooperation among the harshly competitive relations of men with one another.

In the account of creation in Genesis, the author writes of God making mankind in his own image, male and female (Genesis 1,27). He also writes of man being unable to sustain solitude and woman being drawn from man to be his companion, that he may go out to her and become as one body with her (Genesis 2,18-24). If he had written that in the beginning man had come out of woman, that would have been no new thought to anybody. But when he writes that woman came out of man, he completes the circle and sketches a kind of harmony and community intended in creation. He immediately follows up with the observation that conjugal fidelity is the basis for realizing that harmony, and this implies that each marriage looks beyond itself to God, the creator and the end of creation.

In the history of Israel the key theme of covenant is frequently presented as a marriage between God and Israel. Covenant is different from a contract. In the latter there is an exchange of pledges or commitments to quite specific obligations which are spelled out beforehand so that each party to the contract knows exactly what is involved and what his responsibilities are. But in a covenant of alliance or friendship, the commitment is open-ended. It is a pledge of personal loyalty to be sustained in changing and unpredictable circumstances. Marriage, therefore, is a covenant, because it is a total commitment of the persons to each other. It is not to be conditional on certain circumstances.

The Hebrew scriptures give us an interpretation of the history of Israel in which God is forever faithful to the covenant and His fidelity, in spite of Israel's infidelity, keeps creating the possibility of return and reconciliation and growth. The whole book of Hosea is a dramatic account of this element. It is a story of the prophets interpretation of God's love by his own conjugal love. The prophet's fidelity is not only a sign of God's fidelity; it is a sign that helps to effect what it signifies. It is precisely through the kind of life that Hosea lives that God's fidelity becomes a reality for Israel.

The prophecy of Jeremiah takes up the same theme and idolatry is spoken of as adultery (Jeremiah 1-3). The theme also occurs in the prophecies of Isaiah and Ezekiel. It is one of those cases in which, to understand or interpret, one must enter into the reality with one's own experience, and marriage is the basic human experience of what creative, redemptive, saving love is. In a marriage it is experienced both as giving and as receiving. Therefore, every marriage is seen as a precious place of the self-revelation of God in His loving concern for men, calling them to the fullness of personhood which is in the fullness of freedom.

At first sight, it may seem that, whatever other advantages may derive from marriage, freedom is not one of them, precisely because marriage is a commitment. It excludes many other possibilities. In our time the image of "swinging singles" suggests many things the unmarried person is free to do because he has the time and the money and the mobility and does not have to wait for anyone else's consent or cooperation. If we think of freedom as the opposite of commitment, "hanging loose" and allowing no one to make any claims on us, then marriage is not an experience of liberation.

On further reflection, however, it becomes clear that uncommitment is not a restful or happy state. People want to be free in the sense of being able to make their own decisions unhampered. But they can come into that freedom only by making the decisions and to decide is to make commitments. A man can make commitments on an utterly selfish and self-centered basis. But again, experience shows that this tends to lead to depression and anxiety and endless questions as to whether life is worthwhile and whether there is any purpose in life.

People are not convinced about a purpose in life because it is explained to them in words, but only because they experience it. A man experiences a purpose in life when he answers the call of another who values him, calls him by name and engages him in a personal relationship that makes him feel wanted and important and comfortable with himself. Many people go through life afraid of real encounters with people because they have engaged in relationships in which they have been betrayed and devalued. They find it difficult to trust anymore because they feel too vulnerable. They feel they have to hide their nakedness with fig leaves because they cannot be comfortable with what they are.

This, of course, is unredemption. It is what we are concerned with when we speak of the state of original sin—a diffusion of distrust and anxiety and hostility in the relations among men which also makes it very difficult for them to have an open relationship to God or to the world of things, because they cannot believe that God who creates them finds them good. Because we feel devalued and anxious and exposed, we project onto God an aura of harsh judgment and belittling depreciation that is not there.

That is why marriage is destined to be redemptive, to liberate persons out of the enslavement to fear and meanness into a creative freedom of openness to others and to the future. But the very reason that demands that marriage should be redemptive makes it very difficult for it to be so. Marriage partners do not begin out of nothing, they are situated in a history of unfreedom, of unredemption, in a network of human relations that is already rather badly tangled, with personal experiences in which they have already been betrayed and wounded.

In this context, the Church claims that Christian marriage is sustained in a special way as a redemptive experience. When two people marry each other who are reborn in the risen Christ and living by the Spirit which is the breath of God and coming to the encounter with Jesus in his death and resurrection in the Eucharist, then their union will be a living expression and interpretation of the redemptive relation of Jesus with the community of believers. This theme finds its classic expression in the letter to the Ephesians. Husbands and wives are exhorted to love each other with the mutual commitment of Christ and the Church, because their marriage is the sign and celebration of this central mystery of redemption (Ephesians 5,25-33).

It is of interest that the passage does not refer to the love of Jesus for mankind, or his giving himself up for the sake of mankind. It refers to the bond between Jesus and the Church, that is, the community of those who believe in him and respond. There is even a theme running through the imagery of the early Church Fathers that the Church is the new Eve, born from the pierced side of the dying Jesus, the new Adam, who unites himself with her in the marriage bond that they may be one body bringing forth many children of redemption.

Christian marriage, therefore, is made the sign of the fruitful union of Jesus with the community of his followers, and the Church insists that it is such a sign because it is the revelatory experience of that union and helps to bring it about. In other words, the secular reality itself as lived and interpreted by Christians becomes in the fullest sense a sacrament of salvation for those who marry and for their children and for the community. When we assert that it is a sacrament, we also imply that the redemptive experience of marriage that would otherwise seem so difficult and perhaps impossible *is* possible within the Christian marriage because of the love of Jesus for the Church —because he gave himself up to death for "her" and because we, who are the Church, share in his Resurrection.

Many people today ask whether such a view does not seem to reflect very harshly on the sincerity and good faith of those whose marriages appear to have failed. It is clearly on the basis of the above understanding that the hierarchic authority in the Western Catholic church tradition has been unwilling to dissolve consummated marriages between Christians.

The Eastern Churches have had a different practice and the focus of their theology concerning marriage has been slightly different. Instead of being focussed so sharply on the present reality of the union of Christ with the Church in the task of redemption of the world, their understanding of the sacraments is more directed to the future fulfillment of the reign of God. They take up the theme in the gospels and in the Apocalypse (Revelation) in which heaven is compared to a wedding feast and Jesus to the bridegroom claiming redeemed mankind as his own. The sacrament of marriage in its transformation of those involved is the witness of the life of heaven.

The Eastern Churches recognize the perilous circumstances under which marriages actually take place in the time of relative unfreedom or unredemption, while we wait and strive for the reign of God. Therefore they are also willing to acknowledge the dissolution of a marriage that has actually broken down. They allow the parties to remarry and do not exclude them from full participation in the Eucharist and the other sacraments. However, they do not consider a second marriage a sacrament or witness to the reign of God as the first was.

In summary, the Christian understanding of marriage as sacrament is much more than that of a rite of passage marking a definitive phase in people's lives and giving the community's public acknowledgment of it. It is an understanding of marriage as a redemptive experience which draws its power from the death and resurrection of Jesus and which truly effects the liberation of the world from the state of mistrust and anxiety and hostility that we now have into the perfect freedom of the future reign of God.

Notes for Chapter VI

Probably the most helpful presentation of the idea of covenant used in this chapter is that of A. J. Heschel in *God in Search of Man* (Part III) published by Harper Torchbooks. This book is, in any case, of primary interest to anyone who wants to recapture the mode of thought and vision that is shaped by biblical symbolism.

For those who have ready access to a library, the most helpful discussions of marriage as presented in this chapter are in past volumes of *Concilium*, particularly Volume 38 published by Paulist Press and Vol. 55 published by Herder & Herder. Marriage as a sacrament is very fully discussed by Edward Schillebeeckx in *Marriage: Human Reality and Saving Mystery* published by Sheed & Ward.

The practice of Confession as most of us knew it in childhood seems to be changing greatly. Many people who went to Confession frequently no longer do so. Many people who thought the anonymity was an integral part of the sacrament have begun to wonder whether anonymity helps or hinders the main purpose. In some dioceses a communal celebration of the sacrament of Penance without any individual confession of sins has become quite usual, although it was formerly permitted only in a few emergency situations, such as that of soldiers going into battle.

Along with the changing practice, people now find themselves asking questions about the meaning of the sacrament of Penance which never occurred to them before. Some Catholics have suddenly felt the force of the Protestant question, "Why not confess directly to God in the secrecy of your own conscience, because forgiveness comes from God?" Others have asked whether the main purpose of the sacrament is the acknowledgment of sin, or the conversion from sin, or the forgiveness of it by sacramental absolution, or the expiation of it by a work of penance. The thrust of this question is often either to refer back to the previous one, or lead into another, "Would it not be more helpful to confess to a layman who has a charism for receiving a confession of failure and giving the support for conversion and reconciliation, than to confess to a priest who does not have this charism?"

These questions and many more can be answered only in the far broader context of the task of reconciliation in the Church. It will have been apparent in the foregoing chapters that reconciliation is a theme that runs through our entire sacramental practice and theology and is a key factor in the understanding of redemption and grace and Church. The sacrament of Penance is a characteristic celebration of reconciliation, and it is well to consider why we should have such a celebration.

The basic sacrament of repentance, conversion and reconciliation is baptism, the entrance into the Church, because the essence of the Church is reconciliation. In the earliest days of the Church, when those baptized were normally adults, the catechumenate was concerned among other matters with the question of whether there was a genuine conversion in the candidate's life. The baptism had two aspects. It was an acknowledgment of the individual's personal and fundamental commitment to turn from his life of sin and confusion to a life in Christ. It was also the community's reaching out to embrace him and pull him into its midst, so as to make it possible for him really to accomplish that turning in all dimensions of his life. Everybody knew that that was a lifetime project and would not be completed immediately. His baptism was a sacrament whose effect was supposed to spread over his whole life.

The problem soon arose, however, as to what the community was to do in relation to persons who had been baptized and had then left the community in time of persecution or had committed idol worship or had done some morally scandalous thing. The community existed to be a witness of the reign of God by living a holy life, so as to set the world free from its fear, anxiety, suspicion and confusion. It was clear that it really could not fulfill its commitment without excluding those who were not so committed. There had to be a procedure of excommunicating those who did not live the life of Christians. This happened even in apostolic times. Paul gives an example in I Corinthians 5, where he writes to the Corinthians that they must excommunicate from their midst a man living with his father's wife because otherwise the scandal will destroy the community.

The further question then arose for the Christian communities of the first few centuries whether a person who had been excluded from the Church could be rebaptized. Everyone soon agreed that he could not be rebaptized, because baptism is the community's commitment to him and must reflect the fidelity of God Himself. It, therefore, marks him forever as one whom they have accepted into their midst. Instead of baptizing him again, they had a ceremony of the renewal of his one and unrepeatable baptism.

Such a renewal was a public and official ceremony of reconciliation with the Church. The bishop, after assuring himself and the community of the candidate's genuine and fundamental willingness to turn back to a Christian life, would lead him back into the assembly to participate in the Eucharistic celebration. Usually the assurance took the form of the individual's acknowledgement of the sinfulness of his position, his avowal that he wanted to turn away from it and his performance of a public penance directed by the bishop and often lasting quite a long time. The purpose of this penance was to demonstrate to himself and everybody else that he was quite sincere and serious in his avowal and that it was not a momentary change of mood.

In those days it was not customary for everyone to receive the sacrament of penance. In fact, it was regarded as a misfortune that there were any candidates for it at all. It was most generally assumed that the sacrament of penance could be received only once in a lifetime. It is interesting, however, that the evidence we have concerning the theory behind that practice does not suggest that it was limited to one time because God would not forgive people any more than that but only that the limitation of public reconciliation with the community to once in a lifetime was necessary for the stability and common good of the Church. That is, the person was assumed to be forgiven if he turned to God with sorrow, but he had disqualified himself from public participation in the redemptive task of the Church.

At various times and places, the custom crept in of persons coming to the bishop and confessing to him a sin that was not publicly known but which was serious enough to block the person's authentic participation in the redemptive task of the community. The official ritual of reconciliation was extended to these people who publicly identified themselves as penitents by their dress and activities. Moreover, the custom also developed of persons who had not revoked their baptismal commitment in a radical way nevertheless going through the penance ceremony on their deathbeds.

This was just an extension of the practice of Christians at the Eucharistic celebration where, to this day, we all acknowledge our sinfulness. It is a realistic recognition in the course of a Christian life and at the end of it that we have not yet attained the fullness of the reign of God, that there is still a residue of unredemption in our lives.

This recognition came to be further extended in sacramental celebration. Monastic professions were built on the same principle. They were a public celebration of entry into a special class of people devoted to a life as penitents. This practice did not assume that those who sought monastic life were more sinful than other Christians but that they were more alert to sinfulness, more aware of the problems and more concerned to bring about redemption than Christians in general. Christian theology holds that the attitude and commitment of penance relates not only to one's own particular sinfulness but to all that needs to be put right in the world, to the whole vast network of unredemption. When the medieval monastic profession took the form of an entry into the official class of penitents, it was clearly a public commitment to repair the consequences of the evil deeds of others.

From this basis, the Celtic missionary monks also advocated and practiced frequent repetition of the sacrament of penance where there was not necessarily a fundamental repudiation of baptismal commitment involved. The sacrament became the acknowledgment of the failure to realize that commitment in full in all its dimensions.

Modern practice universalised the practice of the Celtic monks and tended to make it so routine that many of us, when instructed in the life and duties of Catholics as children, probably thought that the sacraments of initiation that made anyone a full-fledged Catholic were baptism, confession, holy communion and (if and when the bishop came) confirmation.

When we look back over the history of the sacramental practice, it becomes clearer that the sacrament of penance is basically the celebration of reconciliation of the individual with the Church community. The theology of Christians has always been clear that if a person really repents in his heart of any sin then God has already forgiven him. The relation of the community celebration to this forgiveness by God has raised theological questions at many times.

When we look back to the attitudes and sayings of Jesus himself, we find the classic text of the Parable of the Prodigal Son. The Father of the story never at any time repudiates the younger son. He has already forgiven but his forgiveness cannot take effect, unless and until the son himself returns, that is, until he can bring himself to turn around so that he can meet the forgiveness of the Father. The problem of the story is the elder son who is unwilling.

In the life of the Church it might very well be like this. God always forgives, but the problem might be the self-righteous. In real life this is even more of a problem than in the story, because in real life we do not see God. Our only tangible proof of forgiveness comes from other people in the Church community.

It is more of a problem for another reason also. A true conversion is very difficult and does not happen all at once. As was discussed in the previous chapter, our sinful patterns of attitudes and behavior are closely connected with the fact that we do not feel secure in relation to God as creator nor in relation to our self-image, to other people and to the world around us. Part of the state of sinfulness and confusion that is the effect of what we call original sin is that we feel so devalued that we have an enslaved consciousness and are not very free.

Since it is precisely out of this enslaved and fearful state that we need to be redeemed or converted, it may be assumed that none of us has within himself the freedom to accomplish the conversion, the turning around, alone without support. When Catholic tradition solemnizes and publicly celebrates reconciliation, it claims the sacramental effectiveness in the strict sense. That is, it claims that this celebration, because of Jesus and his community, is a sign that really does bring about what it signifies or represents.

More specifically, what is meant is this: a person presents himself before an accredited representative of the Church community, acknowledges his sinfulness and avows his intention to turn from it in earnest. Solemnly and on behalf of the Church, he is assured of God's forgiveness and his reconciliation with the Church community and is directed into a work of penance that (no matter how insignificant it may be in itself) is the concrete and immediate practical expression of his more subtle inner conversion. Such a sign is able to effect what it signifies because it gives the penitent the support to follow through on his initial desire and decision to convert. It gives him the support of an official ceremony in the name of Christ and the community, the personal encouragement of the encounter with a forgiving person, and the tangible pledge of the directed penance he performs.

Some Catholics may well be apprehensive at this point, wondering what has happened to the remission of the guilt and stain of sin in this explanation. This becomes clear when we recall that God is forever forgiving like the Father in the parable, but that his forgiveness can take effect only if the sinner turns to meet His forgiving welcome. What this means is that the repentance and the forgiveness are two different ways of describing exactly the same event. It is not really that the repentance comes first and after that God forgives. It would be closer to the truth to say the forgiveness comes first and that that is what makes the repentance possible in the first place.

Other Catholics may say that they have never in their whole lives been in a confessional where they have received the personal encouragement of the encounter with a forgiving person. There may be one or more of several reasons for this. The most obvious is that to be open to such an encounter one must be genuinely aware of being a sinner and being in dire need of forgiveness. To go to confession because one is a Catholic and confession is one of the things that Catholics do is not a sufficient basis for such an encounter.

Another possible reason is that it is psychologically and spiritually a very demanding thing, personally, to receive a confession of sin and failure from another person in simplicity and compassion, recognizing the sin and not repudiating the person. To do it one has to have come to terms in a very radical way with the sinfulness and weakness in one's own life, so as to come to an overwhelming trust in God that makes the world and all that goes on in it transparent to the presence of God. It is precisely in this respect that Catholic Christians tend to isolate their ordained priests too much, leaving to them the whole burden of reconciliation within the Church, which belongs to the entire Church.

The strictly sacramental practice of confession, penance and absolution is a visible and ritual celebration of what is assumed to be an ongoing reality in the whole fabric of the life of the community. If it is not such a reality in the community, it is not likely to be realized as a sacrament. This is what is at stake when the topic of "lay confession" is under discussion. The term may refer to the need within the community that persons apologize to one another, accept apologies and truly forgive as the occasion arises. It may also refer to a more or less casual acknowledgment of failures among friends who will engage themselves to do penance for one another, that is, help one another to put things right. It could refer to a more formal and sustained one-to-one relationship in which a lay Christian with a charism for it supports another in a conversion. What is basic is that there must be an ongoing practice of authentic personal reconciliation within the Christian community if the sacrament of penance is to have a truly personal meaning.

Notes for Chapter VII
The sources for the above presentation would be difficult to assemble. For the basic psychological insights the author is indebted to Josef Goldbrunner in *Realization: The Anthropology of Pastoral Care*, published by the University of Notre Dame Press.

Some of the pastoral aspects of penance are very well discussed by Louis Monden in *Sin, Liberty and Law* published by Sheed & Ward.

The historical development of the sacrament has been traced very carefully by Bernhard Poschmann in *Penance and the Anointing of the Sick* published by Herder & Herder. A discussion of the systematic theology of penance is given in *The Sacrament of Penance* by Paul Anciaux, published by Sheed & Ward.

Most Catholics know that the Church reckons the sacraments as seven and would probably list them so that the last has something to do with dying. The numbering of the sacraments dates only from the later Middle Ages and is, in a sense, an arbitrary arrangement. For instance, given the existing practice, orders might have been counted as several sacraments, baptism, confirmation and Eucharist could have been grouped together as initiation, and Eucharist could have been counted again as Sunday celebration, and a third time as viaticum and so on.

Seven is a number, however, that has a meaning beyond its numerical count, and that is the connotation of completion or fullness or perfection. So it was quite suitable that the sacraments should be numbered as seven. It indicates that they embrace all aspects of life and do not mark boundaries between sacred and secular realities. Moreover, it is suitable enough that the seventh sacrament should be connected with death.

There is nevertheless, considerable confusion in the history and practice of sacramental celebrations surrounding grave illness and death. From earliest times the Church has had the custom of anointing in the name of Christ and the community those so gravely sick that there could be assumed to be a danger of death. The purpose of the anointing was clearly two-fold: to bring to bear on the situation all the encouragement and support the Church could offer in the hope that it might contribute to recovery of health, and to bring spiritual strength to sustain the illness with a radiant hope in the resurrection, even if the sickness should lead to death.

There are several important aspects in this. First, there is the clear assumption that illness and suffering in themselves are not salvific or redemptive but must be made so by the Church that is the link with the resurrection. In fact, illness and pain tend to destroy rather than build up human freedom and integrity, and it is only in the mystery of the Cross of Jesus that the Christian sees the possibility of suffering as redemptive. It is not redemptive in itself, but only if and when it calls forth extraordinary love and commitment that purposefully focusses a person's life to its goal in God. Such love and commitment would be expressed first and foremost in the will to overcome the illness and to live, and, only where that is impossible, in the clarity of vision that accepts death for what it is and meets it with confidence in the promise of God.

Secondly, because of the above, there is an insistence on the dignity of the person who is sick as a free and responsible person. The Church is supposed to rally to his bedside and make it possible for him to continue to think and act and order his life as a responsible and free person. In pagan cultures of old this was probably difficult because of the lack of concern to provide adequate nursing and medical care for the sick, unless they were very rich and influential, and the general tendency simply to let the sick die or recover on their own. In today's culture it is generally difficult because of the overemphasis on the technical aspects of medical care which tend to humiliate, devalue and depersonalize the person, so that his need for a sustaining and supporting presence from the Christian community is very great, particularly in hospitals and nursing homes.

This is probably another area where many a Catholic would complain of the way a priest treated an elderly relative in the hospital. Again, one would have to say it is an area in which the laity delegate too much to the ordained priest. The whole ministry of encouraging and sustaining the sick person is essentially a lay ministry which should find its culmination and ritual expression in the anointing by the ordained minister. If the substance of the ministry is not being fulfilled, the sacramental celebration cannot have its full meaning. Moreover, many Catholics have come to associate the anointing of the sick with immediately imminent and more or less certain death. In the anxiety not to frighten them, the priest is sometimes kept away until the appropriate moment for this sacrament is long past.

Apart from the anointing of those sick and in danger of death, there grew up the custom already mentioned in the last chapter, of considering penance as the special sacrament of the dying and of those who, because of old age or other reasons, felt that they should prepare for death. In fact, this was the first extension of the sacrament of penance to persons who had not incurred excommunication. They seem to have thought of it as a renewing of their baptism in preparation for death, which was appropriate enough. Baptism was and is the entry into the passion and death of Christ to come to a new life in his resurrection. There could not be a more appropriate time to renew the experience and reaffirm the commitment than before death, particularly for someone who is vividly aware of not having lived up to the commitment.

However, those who have studied the liturgy and its history and theology protest vigorously that the real sacrament of the dying is viaticum, that is, their special sharing in the Eucharistic communion. It is clear that the last solemn communion has a quite distinctive meaning just as does the first solemn communion which is part of initiation into the community. Every Eucharist is an attempt to reach up to a full encounter with the mind and vision and commitment of the dying Jesus, in the light of his resurrection which we, as a community, have witnessed and been born into. But in most of our Eucharistic participations we are not mature enough personally to penetrate too deeply into the mystery.

The best, and perhaps the only, way to understand death is to die, but to die, not just in the sense of being overtaken by death in spite of one's efforts to escape and look in another direction. It must be rather a death that is willed in the sense of being accepted and becoming personal as the laying down of one's life and bringing it to completion to be surrendered to the Father in total trust. The Christian tries to learn this from Jesus and the focal point of his effort to interpret the personal orientation of Jesus to the Father is his participation in the Eucharist.

There is a sense, however, in which the Christian life is supposed to be the rehearsal for death. And it is not a morbid sense. If a death that is a free completion of life and a surrendering of oneself to the Father is possible in Jesus Christ and for his followers, this gives a personal dignity that enhances the whole of life, because it makes the purposefulness and freedom of a human life real and meaningful. If death must necessarily be a passive experience of being taken over by the inevitable in spite of oneself, then life is after all absurd and freedom just a cruel jest.

In Christ, as we meet him in the Eucharist, we learn the conditions for a free death, and therefore of a free life. In every age Christians have meditated on the life and death of Jesus and seen new aspects. The one criterion that runs through the various styles of spirituality that have sprung from this is the radical commitment to the reign of God. We see in Jesus an all-consuming hunger for the holiness of God to be manifest in a right world where His reign is realized because His will is done and men live in dependence on Him knowing no want, where there is reconciliation and the trial is over and men are delivered from evil.

In our times, the element of this that has been most stressed is the selfless orientation of Jesus as a man for others. At other times what was most stressed was his prayerfulness, his sensitively alert obedience to the will of the Father, his willingness to suffer to attain his goals, his ruthless detachment and readiness to disengage from whatever was not the kingdom of God. All of these aspects are in some sense an anticipation of death, of a death willingly died in answer to the call of the Father. The Eucharist is the community celebration that is central to such meditation and assimilation of the attitudes and values and commitment of Jesus. Viaticum is a participation in that celebration under circumstances most likely to make it maximally fruitful.

Healing and death 93

Of course, the individual could meditate alone on the death and resurrection of Jesus. Here again, the Catholic tradition insists that this is where he needs the support of the community most, and the community should be there beside him making it a moment of high and solemn celebration of the mystery of the Church in its union with Jesus Christ. And again, this carries the strong implication that the moment of death and the time immediately before death should be a time of utmost clarity of understanding and vision for the one who is dying, if this can in any way be attained. He should be given every support to personal dignity and freedom and self-direction that the community of Christians can give him. That surely means that it is a grave Christian duty of the community and its representatives that the technical aspects of hospital care not deprive the patient of the possibility and support for a free, personal and Christian death.

Unfortunately, in our society we keep death hidden. Few people have or seek the opportunity to witness the death of others. They would feel out of place as idle spectators. But this is perhaps because we do not have a Christian understanding of death in which the spectator is not idle at all but represents the active support and encouragement of the community. To witness death, however, places the same sort of demands on a person as the receiving of a confession of sin. It demands that one have come to terms rather radically with one's own approaching death as a dimension of life in the present.

Although we do not usually refer to them as part of the seven sacraments, the funeral rites ought broadly to be so considered. They belong to the "seventh sacrament," that is, the sacrament of completion, because for the Christian they are and must be more than the decent ritual disposal of the corpse. They are the community's confrontation with the mystery in its concrete reality and the community's expression of hope in the resurrection out of its own experience of assimilation into the death and resurrection of Jesus Christ.

Notes for Chapter VIII

For this chapter also, the books of Goldbrunner and Poschmann mentioned in the notes for the previous chapter provide very helpful further insight.

For some secular background, *On Death and Dying* by Elisabeth Kuebler-Ross, published by Macmillan, is an honest presentation of the experience of the dying in their own words.

Concerning the religious rites of death *Concilium* Vol. 32, published by Paulist Press, presents both the theological and pastoral considerations.

From the point of view of the Christian's effort to prepare for death by the way he lives, Pflaum/Standard Witness Book *Through Death to Life* by Mary Perkins Ryan is to be highly recommended. More theological in its language and presentation is the essay by Karl Rahner, *On the Theology of Death*, published by Herder & Herder, to which might be added a more complicated book by Ladislas Boros, *The Mystery of Death*, from the same publisher.

Conclusion

Whether sacraments still make sense to Catholics in a secular age and culture depends largely on whether their outlook is secular and Christian or simply secularistic. It is still true, as we have it from early Christian times, that there are basically two ways of living and thinking and planning. Whichever way we look at life, it is interpretation and we have to judge the truth of it by whether we can live it coherently.

There is a way which is flooded with light, because one looks with hope and courage and freedom into the future and sees it as the welcome of God to men. And there is a way which is darkness because in it men see themselves as their goal so that the future is obscure and threatening because it may or may not come to a happy ending.

The way of light is a way of losing oneself in going out to others only to find that that is not loss but gain. The way of darkness is a way of self-seeking only to find that the self is not after all found and the quest ends in despair.

The way of light is a way of constantly asking about the ultimate meaning of life and pursuing the question at any cost, so that life becomes straightforward and integrated and worth living. The way of darkness is attachment to a multitude of things that are not ultimately important, so that life becomes complicated, exhausting and confused and the everyday pressures and demands of society become intolerable.

In the way of light and life, a man accepts responsibility for himself and others, and he discovers freedom in the commitment that he has made. In the way of darkness and death, a man shifts responsibility onto others and criticizes without helping or sacrificing his own interests, and he finds himself trapped and alienated, anonymous in the crowd and pushed around like an object.

To have real hope and courage for the future, we need the support of a community with a common language of gesture and symbol and action and words. This is what Catholics have built in the sacraments. The Church itself tries to be the great sacrament or visible sign of the presence of Jesus in the world, which it hopes effectively to bring about. By the presence of Jesus here is meant reconciliation, peace and justice for mankind quite concretely in all those ways that now seem impossible because men and nations and classes are hostile and afraid and look only to their partisan interests.

The Church tries to be a community that anticipates the future of mankind and thereby makes that future come about. It tries creatively to project and progressively to realize a society in which all relationships can be of trust, mutual respect and concern for the common good of mankind. To be a Christian is to hold a vocation for the benefit of others, for the redemption of the world from fear and war and injustice and despair.

But the Christian community has long been aware that this is an almost impossible task to sustain, and

Conclusion

that it must rally and support the members and keep their eyes on the goal and on the reason for their hope against all counter-indications in the world. The Christian community is for the radically committed, and the sacraments are its corporate expression of its radical commitment.